THE
LAST DECADE
OF BRITISH RAILWAYS
STEAM

A photographer's personal journey

Haynes Publishing

THE
LAST DECADE
OF BRITISH RAILWAYS
STEAM

A photographer's personal journey

GAVIN MORRISON

First published in August 2013

A catalogue record for this book is available
from the British Library

ISBN 978 0 85733 277 6

Library of Congress catalog card no. 2012955427

Layout by Rod Teasdale

Haynes North America Inc., 861 Lawrence Drive,
Newbury Park, California 91320, USA

Published by Haynes Publishing,
Sparkford, Yeovil, Somerset BA22 7JJ, UK.
Tel: 01963 442030 Fax: 01963 440001
Int. tel: +44 1963 442030
Int. fax: +44 1963 440001
E-mail: sales@haynes.co.uk
Website: www.haynes.co.uk

Printed and bound in the USA by Odcombe Press LP,
1299 Bridgestone Parkway, La Vergne, TN 37086

Contents

Introduction

Over the years I have been fortunate in being asked by various publishers to produce several books, using my photographs. Virtually all have been about particular locomotive classes, or specific areas or lines. It had always been my wish to produce a photographic album covering the pictures I took of British Railways steam, and to record some, but not all, of the experiences I had over these years. Also, the book would be a way of saying a big 'thank you' to all the railwaymen who made it possible.

I had expressed my thoughts to my very good friend John Vaughan, who has produced some excellent books recently for Haynes Publishing, and he must have mentioned it during his dealings with the company. This resulted in an unexpected telephone call from Haynes and the rest, as it is said, is now history.

I must emphasise that this is not intended to be a work full of technical detail about locomotives, or a history of individual railways, as these subjects have all been covered many times before. Therefore, by including a few personal experiences and opinions, I hope I have managed to make it just a little bit different.

Having lived in Yorkshire for most of my life, the selection of pictures will have a slight northern balance, but I did manage to visit a great deal of the country over the years, which I hope the pictures will show.

A little information about how I became interested in railways, I feel is appropriate. It all started in 1943 when I was travelling from Leeds to Glasgow to visit my grandmother, and my father bought me an Ian Allan ABC (which I still have), and suggested I watched out for locomotives and see if they were in the book. Little did he realise what he had started, and what trouble it would cause in the future on family holidays, when all I wanted to do was spend my time at the nearest station when my parents thought there were better things to do. This, my wife claims, is an illness, for which there is no known cure. In the mid-1950s there were only 19 steam locomotives that I had not seen in the UK, and that was when there were about 20,000 of them.

I took my first railway picture in 1943 at St Annes station, of the morning Blackpool–Euston train. The problem was that I fired the shutter when the train was hardly in sight and by the time I wound on I only got the tender and half the first coach on the negative. My father did not consider this a good way of using very scarce film during the war, so my photography ceased until I got my box Brownie in 1949. This was the point where my railway photography started, although cost kept it to a very low level.

The first picture I took was of rebuilt 'Patriot' No 45522 *Prestatyn* at Llandudno station. It was not moving so all the locomotive appeared on the film. I am particularly pleased as I did manage to get it published a few years ago, even if it only appeared 3 x 2in. The Brownie was replaced by a bellows camera, which let as much light through the bellows as it did through the lens, so it was soon replaced.

A big step forward was made when my father allowed me to use his old Rolleiflex, but unfortunately, I fell asleep on a train at St Blazey, woke up at the last minute and got off, minus camera. Fortunately, a very kind passenger handed the camera to me out of the moving train window as I walked down the platform. Much of my time was spent 'shed bashing' in the early 1950s, with the aid of a wonderful little book by Flt Lt Aiden L.F. Fuller entitled *The British Shed Directory*, which gave very accurate instructions on how to get to the sheds, with the final sentence usually saying: "… and a cinder path leads to the shed". I suppose today, it would read something like: "… a tarmac road leads to the depot, on which there are barriers with a security guard and lined with CCTV cameras."

By the mid-1950s, I was starting to get organised with my black & white photography, partly due to the advice given to me by the late Eric Treacy, ultimately Bishop of Wakefield, who was a friend of my father. At that time, he was the canon in charge of Halifax parish church. I made a point of attending evensong, not so much for spiritual guidance, but for the advice given in the vestry after the service, on the box of prints I just happened to have with me. I have always considered his pictures taken in the cutting and tunnels out of Liverpool Lime Street to be the best railway pictures ever taken of BR steam.

He undoubtedly had a very strong influence on my photography and I have always tended to follow his type of work, but never managed to get to anywhere near the same standards. In 1956, I mentioned to him that I was going to try taking railway colour pictures, but was told that this was a waste of time as colour would never catch on for railway photography. I ignored this advice and took my first colour

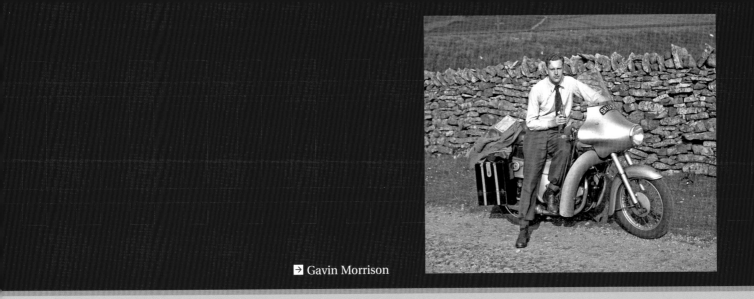

→ Gavin Morrison

slides in 1956 with a Voigtländer Vito B, fitted with a f3.5 lens and a viewfinder, whose content bore little resemblance to what appeared on the slide. This coupled with 8ASA film produced results, which to say the least, left room for improvement. By 1958, I graduated to a Contaflex with an f2.8 lens and used Agfa CT 18 film at 50ASA and stayed using this film virtually to the end of BR steam.

I bought my first motorbike in 1957, which got me all over the country at reasonable cost, and the number of pictures increased dramatically. I was taking colour and black & white at the same time, with the cameras mounted on a bar and it worked well. Nearly all the pictures in the book were taken this way. I carried on doing this two-camera operation until I gave up B/W work about ten years ago. The motorbike era came to an abrupt end when I lost control chasing a train up Shap near Scout Green, and landed in a gorse bush. Four-wheeled transport then took over in the shape of a red VW Beetle, which followed specials all over the country.

By the 1960s, I was producing about 1,500 to 2,000 slides a year, plus the B/W pictures, as well as cine and this continued to the end of steam. Apart from the years immediately after steam finished, I continued at this level of pictures up to the present, although I now only do colour. Today of course, some photographers with their digital cameras seem to go through just as many exposures at a weekend steam gala.

I was working in Leeds in the early 1960s and fortunately my job gave me a fair amount of freedom away from the office. This enabled me to get to know the shedmaster, inspectors, foremen and drivers at Leeds Holbeck shed very well. After several official footplate trips, many of the crews would allow me to ride with them, especially over the Settle–Carlisle line, and occasionally through to Glasgow. Smoke was provided by prior arrangement on occasions, and B/W prints were provided to all concerned. Many of the signalmen, whom I got to know in the area, also did me many favours.

These were fantastic times and I will always be grateful to all the railwaymen who helped me. I could write a small book on everything that happened, but even now I feel many of the tales are better left out of print. Unfortunately, I did not take pictures of the crews at work, watering, coaling and preparing the engines on the shed. It was a wasted opportunity, which I have always regretted. I did not really start getting people in my pictures until I started visiting India about eight years after BR steam ended. In India, you could not avoid getting people in the picture, even if you wanted to.

As the chapters in the book will show, the relentless programme of the elimination of steam progressed through the years and I, together with thousands of other enthusiasts, rushed around the country trying to keep up with events.

I certainly did not achieve all that I would have liked, but there were other matters to take into account. Eventually, it all ended with the biggest traffic jam ever seen at Ais Gill summit on 11 August 1968 to see the passing of the 'Fifteen Guinea Special' with 'Britannia' No 70013 *Oliver Cromwell*. I took several pictures before Ribblehead and just assumed I would beat the train to Ais Gill. By the time I actually got out of the car, the special must have been well past Appleby, so no picture at Ais Gill. All was not lost, as I got some very amusing cine of the solitary local policeman doing his best to sort out the traffic chaos. It did not really matter that I missed the picture as 45 years later, one can still take a picture of *Oliver Cromwell* at Ais Gill.

I thought the world had come to an end when steam finished and I started going overseas and spending far too much time at the recently reopened Keighley & Worth Valley Railway, rather than covering the very interesting (by today's standards) BR scene. By 1974 I had sorted things out and resumed at the same level of activity on BR, as in the steam era.

I can honestly claim, much to my wife's and children's dismay, that I have not given up my railway interest for a day over the last 70 years, and the photography since 1949. The selection I have chosen for this book represents about 1 per cent of my total collection, which I am glad to say is all computerised and I can usually find any picture within half a minute. I dread to think what it would be like if I only had to rely on my brain.

I would like to thank Haynes Publishing for giving me the opportunity to produce this book and for the free hand in its compilation.

I hope you the readers get as much pleasure from the book as I have done in preparing it. I repeat my comment made at the start: it is very much a personal review of my experiences and in no way meant to cover anything technical.

Finally, another thank you to the railwaymen who made so many of the pictures possible.

1959

Looking back in time, 1959 was probably the year, as far as steam enthusiasts were concerned, which was the lull before mass dieselisation, and to a lesser degree, electrification started in earnest.

Steam was becoming scarce in the East Anglia and Kent areas, but diesel locomotives, especially the Type 2 classes, were being introduced on a wide variety of duties. In many cases they only worked for short periods before moving to other areas.

On all the regions, steam still dominated the main express services, although the English Electric Type 4 (later Class 40) was working the Liverpool Street–Norwich trains and some services on the East Coast and West Coast main lines.

Closure of lines was minimal compared with what was to follow in the years to come. Among these were the following:

Beccles–Yarmouth South Town
The Holmfirth branch
Bristol–Radstock–Frome (Western)
The Aberfoyle branch
Hawes–Garsdale
Kilmacolm–Greenock Princess Pier
Oldham–Guide Bridge
Gloucester–Ledbury

Several engine sheds also closed completely, or were rebuilt for diesels including:

Coventry
The three at Great Yarmouth
Melton Constable
Fratton
Faversham
King's Lynn and South Lynn
Walsall
Darnell (Sheffield)

On the locomotive scene, ten steam classes became extinct, the most notable being the unique ex-LNER Class W1 4-6-4 No 60700, and the last 2-4-0 in service on BR, Class E4 (No 62785), which ended its career working Cambridge to Colchester services. Surprisingly, a couple of diesel classes became extinct too, namely the solitary 'Fell' Bo-Bo No 10100, and the one-off Southern diesel mechanical shunter No 11001.

Other notable events were the first 25kV electric passenger service opened in the UK, between Colchester, Walton-on-Naze and Clacton, and the introduction of the electric Class 71 locomotives on the Victoria–Newhaven boat trains. A press trip was run in November, using the first of the future West Coast electric locomotives, No E3001, on a 9¾-mile trip from Wilmslow to Manchester London Road via Style. Another important event for steam enthusiasts was the return to working order of the four Scottish preserved engines.

This was the first year that I took any quantity of colour slides, although I had been taking a few since 1956. I was using a Voigtländer Vito B camera with an excellent f3.5 lens, but with a very inaccurate viewfinder and with doubtful shutter speeds. I used various film types of mixed quality, which overall produced less-than-satisfactory results.

In superb external condition, as was normal for Haymarket (Edinburgh) (64B) locomotives in the 1950s, one of their finest Class A4s, No 60027 *Merlin*, is shown climbing the 1-in-200 gradient from Grantham to Stoke Summit. It passes Little Ponton with the Saturday working, using the stock of the 'Elizabethan'. The headboard is placed in reverse on the front of the locomotive.

It was originally numbered 4486, when delivered new to Haymarket on 13 June 1937. It received its British Railways number 60027 in June 1948, having also carried Nos 588, 27 and E27 in the previous two years. According to records, it covered just over 1,556,000 miles during its career of 28½ years, the second highest for a member of this class. It carried many different liveries, starting with LNER green, followed by blue, purple, BR blue and finally BR green. It was eventually withdrawn from St Margarets (Edinburgh) shed (64A) in September 1965, complete with a yellow stripe on the cabside, prohibiting it from working south of Crewe under the wires.

This was one of the most frequent of the Haymarket A4s to work the non-stop 'Elizabethan' service, from June 1953 to September 1962, but would also have put in many miles hauling other Edinburgh–King's Cross trains, such as the 'Capitals Limited', 'Flying Scotsman', 'Heart of Midlothian', 'Talisman', and others. Generally, the Haymarket Pacifics did not work south of Newcastle except for the A4s, and it was only those fitted with corridor tenders, although they were seen in the south occasionally, after a visit to Doncaster Works. **Date: 5 September 1959.**

'Princess Royal' No 46212 *Duchess of Kent* passes Tebay as it starts the climb to Shap Summit, five miles away. Although this was a Sunday, it was unusual to see a member of this class heading the down 'Royal Scot' in 1959, a 'Princess Coronation' being the normal power. No 46212 had been allocated to all the main West Coast sheds in England during its career, and at the time this picture was taken it was at Crewe North (5A), where it had been since March 1956. It remained there until withdrawn in October 1961, having travelled 1,486,229 miles.

Although it was the last of the class to be built, entering service in October 1935, it was in the first batch to be withdrawn, in October 1961. The position from which the photograph was taken is where the M6 motorway now crosses the railway. **Date: 14 June 1959.**

↑ The south end of Ipswich station is the location for this picture showing the last active Class D16/3 4-4-0, No 62613, and the last member of the famous D16 'Claud Hamilton' class. It entered service in June 1923 and was altered to a D16/2 in 1933, and then rebuilt as a Class D16/3 in 1948. Only three other members of the class received the new BR crest, but with this facing forward, with the lion facing to the right this was a serious heraldic mistake.

The locomotive had been specially prepared to haul the 'Eastern Counties' LCGB special from Fenchurch Street to Cambridge, and from Ipswich to Liverpool Street on the return journey, and it performed well. The tour had a good variety of ex-Great Eastern motive power, which included classes B12, E4, J15 and J69/1. It visited Stoke Ferry, Burnham Market and King's Lynn. **Date: 12 July 1959.**

← The Gresley-designed Class D49, of which 76 were built between October 1927 and February 1935, were known as the 'Shires' and 'Hunts', because of the names selected for the engines. The same boiler as used on the Class J39 0-6-0s was used for these three-cylinder 4-4-0s, as it had proved successful. The design was for secondary passenger work in East and West Yorkshire, the Borders and around Edinburgh and Fife, from which the class seldom wandered.

It is said that the locomotives were disliked by the crews, as they were rough riding, but steamed well. Over the years, many modifications were carried out and they ran with different types of tenders. No 62740 *The Bedale* is shown on the ash pits at York shed (50A) and was one of the few remaining in service in the area by this date. It was withdrawn in August 1960 and the whole class had gone by 1961, having been replaced by Class B1 4-6-0s and DMUs. No 62712 (originally LNER No 246) *Morayshire* has been preserved.
Date: 1 March 1959.

↑ Designed by W.P. Reid for the North British Railway, 32 of these fine 4-4-0s were built at Cowlairs Works at Glasgow between 1913 and 1920, classified as D34 by the LNER. They were named after Scottish glens and will always be remembered for their excellent work over the West Highland line, while based at Eastfield shed (65A). They were limited to 190 tons over this difficult route, which frequently resulted in double heading. In the early years of the class, three-quarters of them were at Eastfield shed for West Highland duties, and even after the arrival of the more powerful Gresley 2-6-0 Class K2s, the two classes dominated the trains on this route until after Nationalisation.

What is remarkable about the 'Glens' is that nine members out of the 32-strong class were only allocated to one shed for their entire careers. This was the case with No 62467 *Glenfinnan*, which is shown here on Thornton shed (62A), where it was allocated for 47 years before being withdrawn in 1960. They were extremely reliable locomotives, and received virtually no modifications. It was recorded that they would often go for two years between general repairs at Cowlairs Works, in spite of the heavy work they had to do on the West Highland line.

Thornton shed at the time of this picture, had an allocation of 94 locomotives, mainly for serving the coalfields of Fife, as well as providing the locomotives for the local passenger services. **Date: 12 April 1959.**

→ In the 1950s and early 1960s, it was not unusual for preserved locomotives to work specials on the main lines. In 1958 and 1959, authorisation was given to return North British Railway 4-4-0 Class D34 No 62469 *Glen Douglas* and Great North of Scotland Railway 4-4-0 Class D40 No 62277 *Gordon Highlander* to working order to haul specials to a major exhibition being held at the Kelvin Hall at Glasgow. Both locomotives were painted and numbered in their pre-Grouping company liveries, the D34 as No 256 and the D40 as No 49, although the latter did not carry the green livery as shown in the photograph, when new. Two other locomotives were also restored: the Caledonian Railway single 4-2-2 No 123, and the Highland Railway 4-6-0 'Jones Goods' No 103.

One of the specials to the exhibition ran from Ayr and is seen near Troon, comprising ten coaches. From a casual observation of the train as it passed, there appeared to be only about ten passengers on it. These locomotives continued hauling specials until 1962, when they were put in the Glasgow Transport Museum. **Date: 11 September 1959.**

◁ Mallaig shed was just big enough to house one locomotive. On this day, Class K2/2 No 61764 *Loch Arkaig*, named in 1933, was in light steam and was allocated to Eastfield shed (65A). Originally, the class worked on the Great Northern main line when they were introduced in 1912, but some were transferred to the Great Eastern section after the arrival of the Class K3s. Over the years, after Grouping, they were allocated all over the ex-Great Northern area.

Around the early 1930s, 30 2-6-0s were transferred to Scotland, most to Eastfield shed to work the West Highland line, which they did, together with the Class D34 'Glens' for more than 20 years. Eventually, some moved to other areas in Scotland. Side-window cabs were fitted to the Scottish locomotives, making them easily recognisable from the rest of the class, which totalled 75. Thirteen were allocated names after Scottish Lochs. No 61788 Loch Rannoch was the last to be withdrawn in June 1961. **Date: 22 July 1959.**

▷ Ballinluig Junction was just over 23 miles north of Perth, on the old Highland Railway main line and was the point where the short branch to Aberfeldy left. One of the ex-Caledonian Railway Class 439 0-4-4Ts, No 55218 allocated to Perth shed (63A), was working the branch on this day and it had just arrived at the junction. A total of 68 of the class were built from 1899, the last of which was withdrawn in 1962. One has been preserved by the Scottish Railway Preservation Society. The branch lasted 100 years, from 1865 until 1965. **Date: 13 June 1965.**

◁ The Great North of Scotland Railway had four 0-4-2Ts, built by Manning Wardle in 1915, for shunting in the docks at Aberdeen. There were two locomotives in each of the two classes; Z4 and Z5. The two classes were the same except that the Z4s, which were the last to be built, were 2 tons lighter. All were allocated to the main GNofS shed at Kittybrewster (61A) Aberdeen, for their entire careers, although it is recorded that No 68191 escaped to Thornton shed for one month in 1942. They were withdrawn between 1956 and 1960 when diesel shunters took over. Class Z4 No 68191 is shown on Kittybrewster shed, having been withdrawn three months earlier. The others were still active, but probably doing little work at this time. **Date: 11 June 1959.**

⬆ By 1959, it had become quite unusual to see an ex-Midland Railway Fowler 4F 0-6-0 working a freight over the Settle & Carlisle line. Between 1911 and 1922, 192 were built, becoming the regular power for freight until the mid-1930s. No 44009, which had been allocated to Carlisle Kingmoor shed for many years, is seen just north of Horton-in-Ribblesdale on the 'Long Drag'. Travelling at about 15mph, one was still able to hear it toiling towards Blea Moor summit 20 minutes later. I doubt if it hauled many more freights on its own over the S&C, although it was not withdrawn until May 1964. **Date: 23 May 1959.**

⬇ There were 125 of these fine Fowler 2-6-4Ts built, the first appearing in 1927. During their careers they operated over most of the LM Region, on local and semi-fast passenger work. The Manchester, Stoke and the West Riding of Yorkshire areas had them allocated for many years. Here, we see No 42413 passing Bradley Junction, just to the east of Huddersfield, at the head of a Bradford to Huddersfield train, which probably continued to Holmfirth, Penistone or Meltham. No 42413 had been allocated to Hillhouse shed at Huddersfield, since Nationalisation at least, until it was withdrawn in May 1964.

Other notable workings for the class were as Shap bankers, when they were allocated to Tebay shed, and working the long Central Wales services from Swansea to Shrewsbury. It is a great shame that one of the class did not make it into preservation, especially as No 42394 of Holbeck shed had hardly done any work following its last visit to the works. The last of the class, No 42410, was withdrawn in 1966. **Date: 27 August 1959.**

↑ Collett 7400 class 0-6-0 pannier tank No 7428 was providing the power for the one-coach Bala to Blaenau Ffestiniog service over the scenic line via Cwm Prysor and Trawsfynydd on this day. The train is in Blaenau Ffestiniog station ready to leave. What is unusual is that No 7428 is still carrying GWR initials on the tank sides, 11 years after Nationalisation. Ninety Class 6400 and 7400s were built between 1932 and 1950. The '64xxs' were fitted for auto-train working and the last of the class was withdrawn in 1965. Three examples have been preserved.

Services on this line ceased in January 1960, but it remained open from Blaenau Ffestiniog to Trawsfynydd to serve the nuclear power station, which has now been mothballed.
Date: 30 March 1959.

↗ On summer Saturdays in the 1950s, there was a through working from Poole to Bradford Exchange. This involved a Southern set of coaches in green livery, coming north one weekend and spending the whole week in the sidings, returning the following weekend. The train was normally worked by a Low Moor (56F) Class B1 and it travelled via Halifax, Huddersfield and Penistone, where it joined the old Great Central main line and then headed south.

Low Moor B1 4-6-0 No 61230, complete with Southern Region coaches, is climbing the steep gradient of 1 in 50 out of Bradford Exchange past Hall Lane, with the help of a banker to Bowling Junction, about a mile away. No 61230 went new to Hammerton Street shed in Bradford (56G) in September 1947 and stayed there until the shed closed to steam in 1958. Except for a short spell at Mirfield (56D), it moved to Low Moor (56F), where it remained until withdrawn in 1962.
Date: 22 August 1959.

→ This picture was taken at Penistone on the old Lancashire & Yorkshire platforms, where ex-Great Central Class C14 4-4-2T No 67445 was running round the coaches before leaving with an afternoon service to Doncaster, via Barnsley Court House and Wombwell. The class consisted of 12 locomotives built by Beyer Peacock, between May and June 1907. Most members of the class put in around 50 years of service, covering a wide area, which included Marylebone suburban services, the Nottingham area, East Anglia, Manchester, and the West Riding of Yorkshire, to name a few.

No 67445 was a Barnsley locomotive at the time of this photograph and was the last to be overhauled at Gorton Works, in August 1954. It was withdrawn in December 1959. This service was discontinued on 27 June 1959, resulting in the closure of stations on the route. Silkstone and Dodworth stations, between Huddersfield and Sheffield, however, reopened on 15 May 1989 and now have an hourly service. **Date: 9 May 1959.**

This was the first year that I really started taking colour slides in any quantity. I mainly used Agfa CT 18 film with a single-lens reflex camera and a f2.8 standard lens, taking around 900 slides in the year. This was before Agfa produced the Gold Star CT 18 film, so the results were rather grainy.

From the steam enthusiast's viewpoint, events were not quite as bad as they could have been, the main event of the year being the completion of the last steam locomotive built for BR, No 92220 *Evening Star* at Swindon Works, unveiled on 18 March.

On the other hand, several classes became extinct. Those on the Eastern, North Eastern and Scottish regions were the A8, B2, B17/6, C13, C14, D30 'Scotts' and the J73s which all went. The last Midland 0-4-4T, No 58086, was withdrawn, and on the Southern Region, the E1/R class vanished. On the Western Region, the 3100 class 2-6-2Ts went and, possibly the most significant, was the last 'Dukedog', No 9017, but this was later preserved, plus some dock tanks. Considering the numbers of EMUs and DMUs entering service, plus the introduction of two important diesel classes (later classified 33 and 37), the steam withdrawals were modest.

A few high-profile events took place, such as the introduction of the Midland and Western DMU Pullman services between London St Pancras and Manchester Central, and London Paddington and Bristol. Another event of particular note was the introduction of the 'Blue Trains' EMUs on the suburban services around Glasgow, north of the River Clyde. This got off to a very bad start however, as after little more than a month the whole fleet had to be withdrawn due to technical problems.

The opening of the 25kV services in September, between Manchester and Crewe, was the start of the West Coast Main Line electrification scheme, which was to take another 14 years to complete, between London Euston and Glasgow.

The closure of the Swansea & Mumbles Railway, the oldest passenger-carrying line in the world, having given 153 years of service, took place on 5 January.

A few steam sheds closed to steam, including Chester (84K), Peterborough (16B), Lowestoft (32C) and perhaps the most significant, Bristol Bath Road (82A).

Some excellent railtours were run using preserved locomotives. These included the last J21 class 0-6-0 working over Stainmore summit. The 'Cumbrian Rail Tour' used the Midland Compound No 1000, which went over the Settle–Carlisle line. Another was the 'East Midlander', as mentioned on page 28.

Line closures were minimal, but included the Dornoch branch in the Highlands, which used 1600 class pannier tanks latterly; the very scenic Bala to Blaenau Ffestiniog line, and the Didcot, Newbury & Southampton route which, in later days, had been using the preserved *City of Truro* on the services. Northwich to Sandbach services ceased, and Barnstaple Victoria Road (GWR) station closed. Possibly the most noteworthy event, in view of how things have turned out, was the reopening of the Bluebell Railway between Sheffield Park, nearly to Horsted Keynes, as well as buying two 0-6-0T engines from the Southern Region. These were P class No 31323 and A1X class No 32655, which was the start of the standard gauge preservation movement.

⬆ This tour was organised by the Railway Correspondence & Travel Society and the Stockton & Darlington Locomotive Society. It provided the opportunity for passengers to travel over the Stainmore line, crossing Belah Viaduct and to climb Shap behind what was to become the last of the famous Class J21s, which operated the line for many decades. The locomotive was No 65033, originally LNER No 876, which had been withdrawn in November 1939 but reinstated due to the Second World War, and then survived to be the last of the class. It was withdrawn in April 1962 and passed into preservation.

The train was sold out, which was no surprise as the locomotive was limited to three coaches. It is shown passing the delightful station at Ravenstonedale near Tebay, which lost its passenger services on 1 December 1952, the line closing completely on 22 January 1962. The station is now a private house and the new road alignment passes over the old trackbed for some distance. The J21 climbed Shap bank without assistance in 13½ minutes and made a fine sight passing Scout Green signalbox. **Date: 7 May 1960.**

⬆ The express services between Leeds Central/Bradford Exchange and Liverpool Exchange were for most of the post-war years worked by Stanier Class 5 4-6-0s, allocated to Low Moor (56F), Bank Hall (27A), and Southport (27C) sheds. Separate portions ran from Bradford and Leeds, which usually combined at Halifax but sometimes at Low Moor. A rare working occurred on this day, with the appearance of 'Jubilee' class No 45552 *Silver Jubilee* of Edge Hill (8A), heading the Bradford portion of an evening express to Liverpool. It is shown entering Lightcliffe station near Halifax, which had its passenger services withdrawn on 14 June 1965.

No 45552 came off the train at Halifax and then worked a parcels service to Huddersfield later in the evening.
Date: 27 May 1960.

⬅ This is a view of the cabside of No 45552 *Silver Jubilee*, showing the chrome-plated numbers. The engine changed identities with No 5642 *Boscowen* on 29 April 1935 and was specially painted in a very high gloss black livery with all handrails, boiler bands, smokebox door handles and other parts chrome plated.

The letters on the nameplate also had a chrome finish. Although the livery changed several times, the locomotive kept the chrome numerals until withdrawn in September 1964, although it is said that some of the original numerals had been lost or stolen and replaced by wooden ones. The locomotive spent its entire career allocated to West Coast Main Line sheds. **Date: 27 May 1960.**

⬆ Bank Hall shed in Liverpool (27A) had three 'Jubilees' on its allocation, between the late 1940s to the early 1960s, namely *Mars*, *Dauntless* and *Glorious*. They were mainly rostered to work the expresses from Liverpool Exchange (closed on 30 April 1977), to Glasgow Central, and the daily 10.30am service to Newcastle via the Calder Valley main line as far as York, returning in the evening. In July 1958, 'unrebuilt' and unnamed 'Patriot' No 45517 was transferred from Willesden and remained at Bank Hall until withdrawn in April 1962 when replaced by 'Jubilee' No 45657 *Tyrwhitt* from Carlisle Kingmoor shed. It became the regular locomotive for the Newcastle diagram and is seen here bursting out of Elland Tunnel, heading east on a frosty day. The Calder Valley services went over to DMUs in 1962 and Bank Hall shed closed in 1966. **Date: 16 February 1960.**

➡ Inside the magnificent Glasgow Central station, which opened on 1 August 1879, is 'Princess Coronation' No 46244 *King George VI*, ready to leave on the 401-mile journey to Euston, at the head of the up 'Mid-Day Scot'. The locomotive was originally streamlined but lost its streamlined casing after being involved in a serious accident near Atherstone in July 1947. At the date of this picture it was only two months since it had received a heavy general repair. During its career of 24 years it was allocated to Camden shed (1B) for 18 of them. It was withdrawn on 12 September 1964 with a recorded mileage of 1,400,154 miles. The last titled run of the 'Mid-Day Scot' was on 13 June 1965. **Date: 12 August 1960.**

⬆ BR Standard 6MT 'Clan' class Pacific No 72003 *Clan Fraser* is making slow progress near the top of the 1-in-75 Shap bank, without assistance at the rear, heading the 14.15 Liverpool Exchange–Glasgow Central express. Initially, the class of ten, five of which were allocated to Polmadie (66A), were used on the Manchester/Liverpool–Glasgow services. These were often heavy trains, which sometimes caused problems for the class. They were replaced by BR 7MT 'Britannias' in 1954. The Polmadie-allocated 'Clans', Nos 72000–72004 were all withdrawn after ten years' service (1952–1962). **Date: 6 August 1960.**

◤ The primary function of Beattock shed (68D; 66F from 1962) was to provide the banking locomotives for the 10-mile climb to Beattock Summit, plus working the Moffat branch. In 1950, it had an allocation of 16, which included six of the Wemyss Bay Caledonian Railway 4-6-2Ts. The last of these was withdrawn in October 1953 when Fairburn 2-6-4Ts took over the duties, helped occasionally by ex-Caledonian 0-4-4Ts. The shed closed in 1967 with the Fairburns still doing the banking, assisted by BR Standard 2-6-4Ts and 4MT 2-6-0s. No 42215 spent ten years allocated to Beattock shed and is seen banking Polmadie rebuilt 'Royal Scot' No 46102 *Black Watch* past Greskine, halfway up the climb. **Date: 4 June 1960.**

◤ Ais Gill Summit, at 1,169ft above sea level, is a familiar location in the railway press today, with pictures of the many specials travelling over the Settle & Carlisle line. Carlisle Kingmoor-allocated 'Jubilee' No 45697 *Achilles*, is seen passing the now-vanished signalbox, at the head of 11 coaches forming a summer Saturday relief to the up 'Thames–Clyde Express'. Carlisle is 48 miles to the north and the train will have been climbing almost continuously at 1 in 100 from Ormside Viaduct, 15 miles away. No 45697 was allocated to Carlisle Kingmoor shed (68A) from 1952 to 1962. Its external condition is typical for the shed's locomotives at the time. It became one of the last four members of the class to remain in traffic, being withdrawn from Leeds Holbeck shed (55A), in September 1967. **Date: 16 July 1960.**

⬆ Class K1 2-6-0 No 62011 is ready to leave Mallaig on the 5.40pm to Fort William, calling at all stations. This station opened on 1 April 1901, seven years after Fort William. The K1s spent ten years working the Mallaig extension, No 62011 being allocated to Fort William from 1952 until 1962, when the Birmingham RC Type 2 (later Class 27) diesels took over.

No 62011 was transferred to the North East of England and survived to the end of steam in the area. The preserved K1, No 62005, is currently a regular performer on this line and has been for many years heading the summer tourist train, 'The Jacobite'. **Date: 13 August 1960.**

⬅ This view is from the footplate of K1 class No 62011 as it left Arisaig station on the 5.40pm Mallaig to Fort William stopping train. It was a very pleasant experience, travelling back on the footplate of the Mogul, although it was quite the roughest locomotive I had ever travelled on. This was in sharp contrast to BR Standard 4MT No 76001 on the outward journey which rode and steamed superbly, and managed to gain seven minutes on the schedule from Fort William, in spite of waiting for me to take a picture at every stop, and also killing two sheep en route.

I was amazed to find out that the driver of the K1 had served 22 years at Mallaig and had never been south of Spean Bridge, ten miles south of Fort William. **Date: 13 August 1960.**

⬆ Mallaig shed has already featured on page 12, where details of the Scottish members of the K2 class were given. Here, No 61784, which was not named, is seen emerging from the single-road shed. In 1925, it was transferred to Eastfield (65A) and then spent 15 years at St Margarets (64A) before returning to Eastfield for a further 15 years. Its last four years were allocated to Fort William before withdrawal in March 1961. By this time there was little work for the class on the West Highland and the extension to Mallaig, and it was not in steam on the shed on this day. **Date: 13 August 1960.**

↑ The 10.15am from Glasgow Queen Street to Fort William is approaching Tyndrum Upper, which opened on 7 August 1894 as Upper Tyndrum, the name being altered on 21 September 1953. It is a couple of miles south of County March Summit, 1,025ft above sea level, and the border between Perthshire and Argyll. Both locomotives seen here went new to Eastfield shed for working the West Highland line; BR Standard Class 5MT No 73077 in May 1955, and Class B1 No 61396 in 1952. They put in ten years' hard work on the route before being transferred away.

No 73077 was withdrawn in December 1964 and No 61396 in August 1965.

In the summer months, this train had an observation coach attached to the rear, which was turned on the turntable at Fort William shed and run round the train for the return working. It was originally used on the pre-war LNER 'Coronation' train, although it was now slightly modified. **Date: 13 August 1960.**

↗ Class B1 No 61076 has just received its last general repair at the ex-North British Railway's Cowlairs Works, situated at the top of the famous incline. It was very much a Scottish member of the class, having been built at the North British Locomotive Co works in Glasgow in September 1946 and spent its entire career allocated to Haymarket and St Margarets sheds in Edinburgh. It was withdrawn in September 1965. On this occasion it was working a train to the Fife coast.

Cowlairs bank was opened on 18 February 1842 by the Edinburgh & Glasgow Railway, which was absorbed by the North British Railway, and was originally rope worked by a steam engine at the top. It used to haul 70 to 80 trains per day at a speed of 14mph. The gradient was between 1 in 41 and 1 in 50 and it was 2,090 yards long, including the 1,040yd tunnel. Trains descended the bank using special brake vehicles at the front. After several incidents, the NBR decided to abandon the rope haulage and use banking engines from 12 December 1907. **Date: 11 August 1960.**

→ The 'White Cockade' tour ran from Glasgow Queen Street to Fort William and back, returning via Callander. It was run as a farewell trip for the Gresley Class K4 2-6-0s, which were built at Darlington in 1937 and 1938 especially for the West Highland line. They operated for 20 years before being transferred to Thornton shed (62A) in 1959, where they only lasted another two years before being withdrawn.

The class consisted of only six locomotives. No 61997 (LNER No 3445) *MacCailin Mor* was rebuilt by Thompson as a prototype for his K1 class in August 1945. No 61995 (LNER No. 3443) *Cameron of Lochiel* was the locomotive chosen for the tour, and was slightly different from the rest of the class, having a left-hand elbow joint steam pipe, resulting in different outer casing. They were extremely powerful locomotives with a 36,598 tractive effort and 5ft 2in coupled wheels, making them ideal for the stiff gradients.

No 61995 is on the turntable at Fort William shed being prepared for the return trip. The name and number plates have a blue background. This loco was withdrawn on 2 October 1961 but this did not turn out to be the last visit of the class to the West Highland line, as the preserved example, No 61994 (LNER No. 3442) *The Great Marquess* has been a regular visitor to the line in recent years. **Date: 18 June 1960.**

⬆ BR Standard Class 4MT 2-6-0 No 76001, which had just been transferred to Fort William shed from Motherwell, pauses at Lochluichart halt on the Mallaig extension with an afternoon train from Fort William. The halt opened on 19 August 1870 as a private stopping place for Lochluichart lodge, but was then opened for public use on 1 July 1871. It was re-sited in 1954. I was fortunate to be travelling on the footplate on this day and the driver spoke very highly of the Standard 4MT, which gave a superb performance. It was the only member of the class to be allocated to Fort William shed. **Date: 13 August 1960.**

⬆ Ex-Caledonian Class 439 0-4-4T No 55224 is in steam outside the single-road wooden shed at Ballachulish. No 55224 would be sub-shedded here from Oban, where it had been allocated in February 1960. It only lasted until September 1961 before being withdrawn. Ballachulish station opened on 24 August 1903 and was at the head of Glen Coe. The 28-mile branch ran from Connel Ferry and closed on 28 February 1966.

Ballachulish was an important location, as it was where the ferry operated across Kinlochleven, which saved about a 24-mile detour by road. There is now a bridge and a by-pass on the main road. **Date: 13 August 1960.**

In the days of photographing northbound steam on Shap around Scout Green, about halfway up the bank one had plenty of warning of an approaching train from the exhaust, which could be seen passing Greenholme, and the sound, depending on the wind direction. This gave plenty of time to wander off to your selected location. The one train this did not apply to was the down 'Lakes Express', which left Euston as a heavy train but by the time it reached Shap, it was reduced to about four coaches of the Workington portion, which ran via Keswick.

It was usually hauled by a 'Princess Coronation' with an Upperby crew, who were keen to get home and the speed with which it often climbed the bank had to be seen to be believed. On this day, the Scout Green signalman commented on the speed, as he knew it was a driver with a reputation for not hanging about, so I asked him to phone his colleagues at Tebay and at the summit, to see what times they had recorded the train passing. The times can only be regarded as very approximate, but it was clear that it had averaged over 60mph on the climb. The locomotive was No 46252 *City of Leicester*.

The train was originally named on 11 July 1927, but ceased during the Second World War. It was reintroduced on 5 June 1950 and ran until 28 August 1964, but photographs of it carrying the headboard seem to be rare. **Date: 6 August 1960.**

The return to working order of Midland Compound No 1000 in 1959 was a great event for enthusiasts. Full advantage was taken of its availability for specials by the main tour operators of the day. It was painted in Midland Crimson Lake livery and looked superb.

Forty Deeley Compounds were built between 1905 and 1909. The original five engines were rebuilt between 1914 and 1919 and eventually a further 195 were constructed by Henry Fowler. The Railway Correspondence & Travel Society organised the 'East Midlander No 4' tour, which used the locomotive from Nottingham Victoria to Oxford and back. Even seven years before closure, Nottingham Victoria presented a sorry sight. **Date: 11 September 1960.**

The RCTS's 'East Midlander No 4' tour is at Oxford station during a locomotive change, giving the rare sight of a Midland Compound alongside a Great Western Class 4300 Mogul. No 7317 was in ex-works condition and performed very well on the journey to Eastleigh, reaching speeds in excess of 70mph around Winchester. **Date: 11 September 1960.**

⬆ In 1960, the Worth Valley line was just one of the many branches around the country providing a service which was little used, but costing the railways far more money than it generated. When this picture of the auto train was taken at Keighley, departing for Oxenhope with Ivatt 2-6-2T No 41326 in charge, neither the train crew, nor indeed anybody else, could ever have guessed how things were going to turn out for the line in ten years' time. The history of the start of the preservation group has been well documented many times and the result is there for all to see today.

The branch trains shared platforms at Keighley with the ex-Great Northern line trains to Bradford and Halifax, but these ended in 1955. Passenger services on the branch continued until 1962. In the latter days of steam operation, Manningham shed at Bradford had three auto-fitted Ivatt 2-6-2Ts allocated, one of which was sub-shedded to Keighley shed, just north of the station. **Date: 3 June 1960.**

↑ The Midland main line north of Bingley to Thwaites, just outside Keighley, was four tracks, and Marley Junction was about mid-way. WD class 2-8-0 No 90236, allocated to Low Moor shed at the time, is heading a local afternoon pick-up freight from Laisterdyke to Skipton, which would have travelled via the Idle branch to Shipley. There are only two tracks today, which are electrified for the excellent Aire Valley services. To the left of the picture, a dual carriageway runs parallel with the line. 'Austerity' No 90236 was withdrawn on 12 August 1967. **Date: 9 July 1960.**

1961

I spent a lot of time around my home territory of West Yorkshire during this year, as I could see the diesel invasion was imminent and I wanted to make the most of the A3s working Scottish expresses, as well as the Pacifics on the Leeds–King's Cross services. One casualty in the area from the steam enthusiasts' point of view was the introduction of the Trans-Pennine DMUs on the Hull–Liverpool trains.

Probably the most significant development in 1961 though, was the arrival of the 3,300hp 'Deltics' from English Electric's Vulcan Foundry. Twenty-two of these 100mph machines were to replace 55 Pacifics on the East Coast Main Line. The first time one appeared in West Yorkshire was on 18 July, when No D9003 *Meld* arrived at Leeds Central with a test train, prior to their introduction on the 'West Riding Limited'.

A host of new diesel classes appeared at this time including the Birmingham RCW Type 3 for the Southern and the 'Western' and 'Hymek' diesel-hydraulics for the Western Region. These were to replace steam in the West Country and west of Cardiff with 500 diesels on the Western Region replacing 1,100 steam locomotives. In Scotland, the Type 2s (later Class 27) were introduced and the AL5 ac electrics (later Class 85) arrived on the West Coast Main Line. Further electrification took place on the Southern Region, namely Sevenoaks–Dover Priory and Ashford to Maidstone. Electric services also started on the London, Tilbury & Southend services.

Prototype classes appeared during the year, the most interesting of which was gas turbine No GT3, which ran trials over Shap, as well as on the Great Central main line and in other areas, but its career was short, ending in 1962 after just two years. No D0280 *Falcon*, the prototype of the Class 47s, arrived on the scene, as did the all-white-liveried *Lion* which worked on the Western and Eastern regions.

From my viewpoint the most memorable visits in the year were to the Somerset & Dorset line, and to a lesser degree to the Port Road to Stranraer. Both were superb railways full of character, but of course, there was far more traffic on the S&D, especially on summer Saturdays. Other enjoyable events were some excellent rail tours, which I have illustrated, as well as two memorable footplate rides.

There was some good news for the steam enthusiasts, in that the Bluebell Railway extended to Horsted Keynes, and the narrow gauge Welshpool & Llanfair preservation project took delivery of the 0-6-0T *The Earl* from Oswestry Works, plus some rolling stock.

There was also the bad news: the 'Golden Arrow' was steam hauled for the last time on 11 June, and the end of steam passenger services on the London Transport Metropolitan Line took place on 9 September. The most significant line closure was the Midland & South Western Joint Railway, although three short sections remained open for freight.

By the end of the year, there were significant numbers of under-utilised diesels around, which would have major consequences on the steam stock the following year. Significant casualties in 1961 were the elimination of the Class A2/1 and A2/2 Pacifics, together with the withdrawal of the first two 'Princess Royals'.

In the early 1960s, I used to supply the Public Relations and Publicity department of the North Eastern Region at York with photographs, so my requests for occasional footplate trips did not fall on deaf ears. On this day I was given permission to travel from Leeds to Newcastle and return; outwards on the down 'North Briton' and returning on an up Liverpool express hauled by an English Electric Type 4 (Class 40) diesel, which did not please me very much at the time.

However, there was the bonus of travelling by the long-closed route via Ripon and Wetherby. As can be seen by the superb external condition of the Neville Hill-allocated Class A3 No 60086 *Gainsborough*, considerable effort had gone into the cleaning for my trip. The excellent mechanical condition of No 60086 became apparent as we headed north of York at around 80mph. The ride was almost like being in a car. The picture was taken at Leeds City before departure.

The 'North Briton' first ran as a titled train on 26 September 1949 with the last run being on 4 May 1968. There was a very stable allocation of A3s at Neville Hill from the very late 1940s, *Gainsborough* arriving in February 1949 and remaining there until it was withdrawn on 18 November 1963. **Date: 25 March 1961.**

⬆ In the early 1960s, the clean Class A4 Pacifics from King's Cross shed (34A) were almost daily visitors to Leeds Central station. It was a dirty, draughty station in its latter years, hardly suitable for the upmarket clientele, who patronised the Pullman services of the 'Yorkshire Pullman' and the 'Queen of Scots'. The station closed on 29 April 1967, when all services moved to Leeds City.

The 12.30pm to King's Cross was a regular A4 working and No 60025 *Falcon* is ready to depart and climb the short 1 in 100/50 gradient to Wortley South Junction. **Date: 24 April 1961.**

◤ In February 1960, Holbeck shed at Leeds unexpectedly received an allocation of two Class A3 Gresley Pacifics, followed later in the year by several more. They were transferred from Gateshead and Heaton sheds in Newcastle, where they had been made redundant by the diesels. They were sent to work the Scottish expresses including the sleepers and to replace the rebuilt 'Royal Scots', which had almost monopolised the services for around 16 years.

Most of those transferred were not in very good mechanical order and it took the crews a little while to adjust to them, but they soon took to the comfortable cabs and their free steaming. Their reign was very short, only about 18 months, except for No 60038 *Firdaussi*, before the 'Peak' diesels arrived.

The A3s from across the city were generally in much better condition and it was common for Holbeck to borrow them, as their workload was diminishing. This was the case on this day when No 60074 *Harvester*, which had been at Neville Hill shed for ten years by this time, was working the down 'Thames–Clyde Express', seen passing Dent with the down train. The dilapidated snow fences can be seen in the background. **Date: 8 April 1961.**

◀ After the arrival of the A3s at Holbeck shed, the rebuilt 'Royal Scots' still occasionally worked the Scottish expresses. On this day, No 46109 *Royal Engineer* is seen from Bingley Junction signalbox at Shipley, heading north with the down 'Waverley', which operated as a named train from 17 June 1957 to 28 September 1968. After rebuilding in October 1943, No 46109 remained allocated to Holbeck shed until withdrawal on 29 December 1967. **Date: 20 April 1961.**

⬆ The Laisterdyke to Skipton pick-up freight has already been illustrated on page 31. Here, it is seen again, ready to leave Shipley at Bingley Junction with Low Moor-allocated Class J39 0-6-0 No 64801 in charge. The J39 put in its last 19 years' service around the West Riding of Yorkshire. This part of the Shipley triangle (Bradford to Skipton) is now single track. **Date: 10 May 1961.**

⬇ Ex-Midland 4F 0-6-0 No 44170, allocated to Stourton shed in Leeds, has just had an overhaul at Horwich Works. It is shown taking the Copy Pit line at Hall Royd Junction at Todmorden, with a local freight for Lancashire. It would be banked to Copy Pit Summit, the banker coming on at Stansfield Hall Junction, which was part of the Todmorden triangle, and which is due to be reinstated in the near future, after being closed since 1973. The tracks on the right form the main line to Manchester Victoria. **Date: 14 June 1961.**

↑ Ais Gill Summit, 1,169ft above sea level, has become one of the most photographed locations in the country in recent years, attracting hundreds of enthusiasts to photograph the steam specials over the last three decades. It was very different back in 1961, as one was unlikely to meet another photographer during the whole day, when there to see the procession of freights, as well as the Scottish expresses. Late on one Saturday evening, Newton Heath (26A) 'Crab' 2-6-0 No 42726 is making good progress (about 25mph) with an up freight from Carlisle to Lancashire.

At Hellifield, it will take the line to Clitheroe and Blackburn. No 42726 was allocated to Newton Heath for 18 years before being withdrawn in October 1962. The 'Crabs' were regular performers on freight duties over the Settle–Carlisle line at this time. **Date: 13 May 1961.**

→ Another view of an ex-LMS Hughes 'Crab', this time No 42899 of Carlisle Kingmoor shed in ex-works condition, as it approaches Beattock station and yard with an up freight. It was only when they were ex-works that one was likely to see them in clean condition. The Moffat branch seen on the right lost its passenger service on 6 December 1954, but freight services continued until 6 April 1964. The shed had a small allocation of mainly Fairburn 2-6-4Ts at this time, which did the banking duties up the ten-mile climb to the summit, at 1,015ft. **Date: 20 May 1961.**

I negotiated an official footplate trip from Preston to Carlisle, on a Manchester–Glasgow express. It did not turn out quite as I had hoped, because the locomotive was 'Jubilee' No 45642 *Boscawen*, which was in poor condition both mechanically and externally. I believe the load was only around eight coaches, which should not have presented any problems, but we needed all the recovery time built in to the schedule to record a slightly late arrival at Carlisle.

While *Boscawen* steamed fairly well, it was alarmingly rough at speeds around 60mph and I was quite glad to get off at Carlisle, feeling rather sorry for the crew who were working through to Glasgow Central. No 45642 had a long association with Newton Heath shed (26A), being allocated there from 1940 to withdrawal on 9 January 1965. When built at Crewe Works in 1934, it emerged as No 5552 *Silver Jubilee* carrying a special high-gloss black livery with chrome fittings, raised chrome cab numerals and nameplate letters. On 29 April 1935, it became No 5642 *Boscawen* when the two locos permanently exchanged identities. This picture from the cab was taken as we approached Carnforth station, just as Stanier Class 5 No 45368 was leaving with an up freight. **Date: 17 May 1961.**

In the summer holiday period, several trains were run from the north-east mining areas, taking people to the west coast resorts, especially Blackpool. These trains travelled over the Stainmore line (summit height 1,370ft), through Kirkby Stephen East to Tebay, where locomotives were changed. The trains were frequently double headed, usually by locomotives from Bishop Auckland shed, which by this time were standard BR 4MT or 3MT 2-6-0s, or Ivatt 4MT 2-6-0s. Here, a Newcastle to Blackpool train is approaching Tebay, headed by BR 3MT No 77003 piloting Ivatt 4MT No 43126. Passenger services between Kirkby Stephen East and Tebay ended on 1 December 1952, although the line remained open until 22 January 1962. **Date: 5 August 1961.**

Class B16/2 4-6-0 No 61438 had just received its last general repair one week before this picture was taken on Darlington shed (51A). There were seven B16s modified as B16/2s; the reason for the part rebuilding was to make them more suitable for fast freight workings. No 61438 spent the vast majority of its career allocated to the York and Hull areas, entering service on 17 January 1923 and lasting until 29 June 1964. **Date: 11 October 1961.**

◀ One of the best railtours of 1961 must surely have been the 'Borders Rail Tour', organised by the West Riding Branch of the Railway Correspondence & Travel Society. Starting from Leeds City, 'Princess Coronation' No 46247 *City of Liverpool* hauled the special over the Settle and Carlisle line to Carlisle, covering the 17.25 miles from Hellifield to Blea Moor in 18 minutes 38 seconds. Two B1 class 4-6-0s took the train to Hawick via the Waverley route, where preserved ex-North British Railway Class D34 No 256 *Glen Douglas* and J37 0-6-0 No 64624 were waiting to take over for a trip around the Borders lines, ending at Tweedmouth. From there, Class A1 4-6-2 No 60143 *Sir Walter Scott* hauled the train to Newcastle and finally, Neville Hill Class A3 No 60074 *Harvester* completed the trip back to Leeds. The cost for the 405-mile trip was about £3.

Glen Douglas and the J37 are seen near Earlston on the Greenlaw branch, which originally joined the East Coast main line at Reston, but was severed by the floods in 1949. The 'Glen' is now in the new Strathclyde Museum in Glasgow while the J37 was withdrawn on 17 January 1966 and later broken up. **Date: 9 July 1961.**

⬆ The RCTS 'Borders Rail Tour' is seen crossing the River Tweed, on the beautiful Leaderfoot Viaduct, just before the Greenlaw branch joined the Waverley route. The viaduct is now a listed structure and can be seen from the A68 road. **Date: 9 July 1961.**

⬇ The Eyemouth branch left the East Coast Main Line at Burnmouth. It opened on 13 April 1891, when the town was a very busy fishing port. The line was closed by floods on 13 August 1948 and reopened on 29 June 1949, eventually closing to all traffic on 5 February 1962. By the date of this picture, a single coach was all that was needed to cater for the few passengers. The locomotive, Class J39 No 64917, was provided by Tweedmouth shed and it remained in service until 3 December 1962. **Date: 15 July 1961.**

⬆ By 1961, it had become rare to see the combination of an ex-LMS 2P piloting a 4F 0-6-0 on the S&D but, much to my surprise and delight, No 40569 burst out of Chilcompton Tunnel with No 44422 behind it, heading for Masbury Summit. Both locomotives were allocated to the line at Nationalisation, No 40569 staying until withdrawn on 7 October 1961, while No 44422 was eventually moved away, ending its BR career in May 1965.

When I got back to my car, which I had parked on the road above the tunnel, a local man, who had been watching me wandering around, informed me that there were a lot of poisonous adders about. He said they were usually on the railway embankment, so I am glad he told me after I had taken my pictures, otherwise I would never have got some of my favourite S&D slides!
Date: 12 August 1961.

◥ Many photographic albums and historical books have been produced about the 71 mile Somerset & Dorset Joint Railway, which was a main, but cross-country line with a character of its own. The line opened on 4 August 1869 and it was particularly noted for its steep gradients over the Mendips, between Radstock and Evercreech Junction, as well as the dreadful single-bore tunnels with no ventilation.

There were several miles of 1-in-50 grades, so it is no surprise that double heading was the norm, except for light local workings. The motive power was mainly LMS designs, with the 4F 0-6-0s and 2P 4-4-0s predominating for many years. A few Stanier Class 5s were allocated after the war, followed by the BR Standards.

Special mention should be made of the 11 S&DJR 7F class 2-8-0s designed by Fowler and James Clayton. The first batch of six was built by Derby Works in 1914, followed in 1925 by a further five by Robert Stephenson & Co Ltd, fitted with larger boilers. These 2-8-0s were built for working freights, which they did with great success. After the Second World War they were used on passenger trains on summer Saturdays, avoiding double heading in some cases. They never left the line, but were all withdrawn by 1964. Fortunately, two survive in preservation.

Class 2P No 40700 was allocated to the line before Nationalisation and survived until 14 July 1962. Here, it is seen leaving one of the twin single-bore tunnels at Chilcompton, piloting BR Standard 5MT No 73086 *The Green Knight*, which was on loan to Bath Green Park shed for the summer, from Stewarts Lane in London (73A). The train is a morning, Birmingham New Street to Bournemouth West express. **Date: 9 September 1961.**

◀ The beginning of the end of the S&D was when the Western Region took control of the line in 1958. Their objective seemed to be to divert traffic away and ultimately close it. This they eventually did in 1966. At the end of the summer timetable in 1962, all through express services were diverted away from the line. Prior to that, one or two ex-GWR Collett 0-6-0s appeared, giving this rare combination of 2200 class 0-6-0 No 3210 piloting ex-S&DJR 2-8-0 No 53806 on a northbound express. The train is passing Masbury Summit at 811ft, with what was probably the SO Exmouth–Cleethorpes train. **Date: 12 August 1961.**

⬆ This picture shows the classic S&D summer Saturday combination of the late 1950s and early 1960s. Class 2P No 40564 is piloting 7F 2-8-0 No 53806 on the second half of the climb, from Evercreech Junction to Masbury Summit, on the approach to the twin bore tunnels at Winsor Hill, two miles from the summit. The train is the 11.12am Bournemouth West to Sheffield, with the 4-4-0 having been attached at Evercreech Junction. No 40564 was another member of the class to spend many years on the line, being allocated before Nationalisation and lasting until 27 January 1962, although it had probably been in store during the winter months for several years. No 53806 was one of the Robert Stephenson locomotives and survived in traffic until 28 December 1962. **Date: 26 August 1961.**

These handsome K class Moguls were designed by Robert Billinton for the London, Brighton & South Coast Railway. He initially ordered five of them to be built at Brighton Works, in February 1913. After trials with the first two, modifications were made and the others were constructed. One of the reasons for the class was to speed up the acceleration of freight trains from stops in the London areas, to avoid holding up the suburban services. The freights were mainly in the hands of C2X class 0-6-0s, which although powerful enough, were slow off the mark.

Eventually, there were 17 members of the class built between 1913 and March 1921. They were allocated across most of the main LBSCR sheds and repaired at Eastleigh in the 1930s, but as from 1954, Ashford Works undertook the overhauls until it closed, when Eastleigh took over again. They proved to be sturdy and reliable locomotives and were used on heavy troop trains during the war years. No 32353 is shown on Eastleigh shed after overhaul at the works and was the last of the class to receive a general repair. It came as a surprise when all the class was withdrawn in November and December 1962, as several were in good condition. Apparently the reason was that the Southern Region had a target to meet for withdrawals in the year. **Date: 17 August 1961.**

Maunsell designed the impressive W class 2-6-4Ts for cross-London transfer freight workings. There were 15 in total, the first batch of five being built at Eastleigh in 1932, followed by the others at Ashford in 1935/36. They were three-cylinder locomotives with a high tractive effort and good braking. The 2,000 gallon water capacity was adequate for the short distances.

After the diesels took over their duties in the early 1960s, they were transferred. One shed to receive them was Exmouth Junction (72A), where they were used to bank trains from Exeter St David's to Central station, up the 1-in-37 bank. This did not last long and the others did little work. No 31911, in clean condition, is shown outside Eastleigh shed. The first to be withdrawn was in 1963 and the class became extinct in 1964. **Date: 17 August 1961.**

↑ At the end of 1951 and early 1952, Southport shed (27C) received an allocation of five new BR Standard 4MT 4-6-0s for secondary passenger duties around Lancashire and via the Calder Valley route to Yorkshire. No 75018 is seen on the water troughs between Luddendenfoot and Sowerby Bridge, on the 4.37pm semi-fast from Manchester Victoria to Bradford Exchange. No 75018 stayed at Southport until May 1963 and was then transferred five times, before being withdrawn on 21 May 1967. **Date: 23 June 1961.**

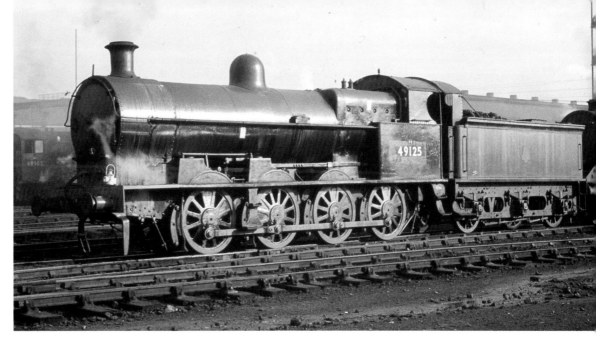

→ Ex-works 'Super D' No 49125 is on Crewe South shed, which by this date must have been one of the last to be repaired at the works. It had been allocated to Bescot shed (3A) since 1954, but it only lasted another ten months before withdrawal on 11 August 1962. **Date: 21 October 1961.**

← The first Ivatt Class J6 0-6-0 entered service in August 1911. The class worked all over the Great Northern Railway lines and they were a familiar sight in West Yorkshire for 50 years. Still in steam, No 64277 has only one day left in service and has probably performed its last duty, as it simmers in the yard outside Copley Hill shed (56B). It was withdrawn the following day with No 64226, making the class extinct. **Date: 19 June 1961.**

→ At Beattock shed two of the Pickersgill ex-Caledonian Railway 4-4-0s, Nos 54502 and 54507, had obviously been in store for some time. No 54507 was allocated to Stranraer and No 54502 to Dumfries. The shed foreman told me that one of them was being considered for preservation, but nothing happened. No 54502 had been officially withdrawn on 29 September 1959 and the other on 21 September 1959, nearly 18 months before this picture was taken. **Date: 20 May 1961.**

↑ This was another significant day on the ex-Somerset & Dorset line, as it was the last day the 2P 4-4-0s piloted the expresses over the Mendips. Long-time favourites on the route, Nos 40564–40569 and 40700 were used in the morning with northbound trains, but then newly allocated to Bath Green Park shed BR Standard 4MTs 4-6-0s piloted the expresses south.

This class was not new to the line, as Nos 75071 and 75072 had been at Bath Green Park since 1956, as well as others, but they nearly always seemed to be used on the local stopping trains. The 4-6-0s were fitted with double chimneys in 1960 and 1961. In BR lined-green livery, No 75023 makes a spectacular departure from Bath, piloting Bournemouth allocated 'unrebuilt' 'West Country' No 34041 *Wilton*, in terrible external condition on the down 'Pines Express'. This named train was introduced on 7 May 1928 and was reintroduced after the war, on 23 May 1949. The last time it ran as a named train was 4 March 1967, although its final trip via the S&D was on 8 September 1962, hauled by BR 9F No 92220 *Evening Star*. **Date: 9 September 1961.**

↗ Inter-regional trains from the North, heading for the Hampshire and Dorset coastal resorts, usually changed locomotives at Oxford. Southern Region locomotives, allocated to Bournemouth shed (71B), were regularly diagrammed to work out and back with morning departures. Other diagrams involved Western Region locomotives, usually 'Hall' class 4-6-0s, but occasionally 'Granges', which worked through to Bournemouth and returned the following day.

The Birkenhead to Bournemouth express is just about to leave Eastleigh station, hauled by an immaculate 'Modified Hall', No 7911 *Lady Margaret Hall*, which was allocated to Oxford shed (81F) for 21 years before being withdrawn in December 1963. **Date: 15 August 1961.**

→ One of Maunsell's magnificent N15 class 'King Arthurs', No 30773 *Sir Lavaine*, is looking well cared for, as it prepares to leave Eastleigh station with an evening stopping train for Portsmouth. It entered service in July 1925 and was allocated to both the South Eastern and Western divisions of the Southern during its long main line service, and is recorded as having covered 1,296,365 miles. In spite of its clean appearance, its days on main line work were over, as it was withdrawn five months after this picture was taken. **Date: 15 August 1961.**

↑ The 'Lord Nelson' 4-6-0s, of which there were 16 members, were designed by R.E.L. Maunsell and entered service between August 1926 and November 1929. They were built to haul 500-ton trains on both the Eastern and Western divisions of the Southern Railway. The class received many modifications, from both Maunsell and his successor, O.V.S. Bulleid, which altered their appearance considerably. In their latter years they worked the Southampton Docks boat trains, but by the early 1960s the Southern Region was awash with Bulleid light Pacifics, so they were withdrawn. No 30864 *Sir Martin Frobisher* is at the coaling stage at Eastleigh shed (71A), with only four months left in service. It still carries the first lion-and-wheel emblem on the tender, and never received the second version. **Date: 15 August 1961.**

↗ For a class of 289 locomotives, the J39 0-6-0s do not seem to have appeared in books and magazines very frequently. The first one, LNER No 1448, later BR No 64700, entered service on 28 September 1926, with the last, No 3098 (BR No 64988) on 21 August 1941. All were built at Darlington Works except for a batch of 28, which was built by Beyer Peacock. They were allocated throughout the Eastern, North Eastern and Scottish areas and were very much mixed-traffic locomotives, very similar to the Midland 4Fs.

   In the days when there were four tracks through the centre of Wakefield Westgate station, No 64796 passes on the down centre road with a rake of empty coal wagons, heading for the yards at Ardsley. After six years allocated to Great Eastern sheds, it was moved to Ardsley shed in 1936 and remained in the West Riding of Yorkshire until withdrawn on 13 December 1962. **Date: 24 August 1961.**

→ When there were direct routes to Bradford Exchange from Wakefield Westgate via Batley, Morley Top or by the triangle at Copley Hill, the expresses from King's Cross to Leeds Central used to split off the Bradford portion at Wakefield Westgate. The main portion continued to Leeds with a Pacific or V2 class 2-6-2. The Bradford section in the 1960s usually had a Class B1 4-6-0 or a Fairburn 2-6-4T. On this day, Class A3 No 60111 *Enterprise* had arrived from King's Cross, and local B1 No 61296, which had been at Bradford and Wakefield sheds since new in March 1948, took over. It is seen departing with the three coaches for Bradford. **Date: 24 August 1961.**

⬆ One of the main marshalling yards along the Calder Valley main line was between Sowerby Bridge and Hebden Bridge, at Mytholmroyd, about midway between the two towns. No doubt it was originally situated here, because it would be able to cope with traffic taking the Copy Pit line at Hall Royd Junction to East Lancashire, as well as that destined for the Manchester area. It was served by Sowerby Bridge shed (25E then 56E), which in later years, had an allocation of WD 2-8-0's, and before that, Fowler 7F 0-8-0 'Austin 7s', with 0-6-0T 'Jinties' for shunting the yard.

The shed was about four miles to the east of the yard, which involved a lot of light engine movements between the two sites. Here, we see an example of two WD 2-8-0s, Nos 90675 and 90673 heading for the yard and passing over Luddendenfoot water troughs. No 90673 was a Sowerby Bridge locomotive at the time and lasted until 14 March 1964, while No 90675 was at Lostock Hall shed, and survived until 9 April 1966. Sowerby Bridge shed closed in 1964. **Date: 20 April 1961.**

↖ One of the 244 Drummond 'Jumbo' 2F 0-6-0s, No 57375, was involved in a railtour around Wigtonshire, together with the preserved ex-Great North of Scotland Railway, Class D40 4-4-0 No 49 *Gordon Highlander*. The special is shown at Glenluce, returning from a trip down the Whithorn branch, which had lost its passenger services on 25 September 1950, with the goods services finishing on 5 October 1964. Glenluce closed on 14 June 1965, with the closure of the 'Port Road' from Dumfries to Dunragit Junction on that date.

Later in the day, ex-Caledonian Railway 2F class 0-6-0 No 57375, which had been allocated to Stranraer shed since before 1950 and normally sub-shedded to Newton Stewart, piloted the Class D40 from Dunragit to the summit at milepost 16½, five miles north of Glenwhilly station on the line to Girvan and Ayr. No 57375 was withdrawn in January 1963. **Date: 2 September 1961.**

↖ A total of 935 Johnson Midland 2F and 3F 0-6-0s were built between 1875 and 1908, and the last one was withdrawn in 1964. Class 3F No 43585, seen here, was on the Hellifield shed allocation since before 1950 and was used as the station pilot, before it was withdrawn on 11 August 1962. **Date: 4 November 1961.**

The Last Decade of British Railways Steam

⬆ This view was taken from the signalbox steps at Dent. Class 5 No 44790, of Carlisle Kingmoor shed, and obviously recently ex-St Rollox Works, is approaching the station, on the 15.30 local service from Bradford Forster Square to Carlisle. In the loop is WD 2-8-0 No 90635, on a Widnes to Long Meg Quarry working. In the background can be seen Arten Gill Viaduct with Wold Fell providing the backdrop. No 44790 was based at Kingmoor for more than 14 years before withdrawal on 9 April 1966, while the 'Austerity', of Wakefield shed, which was unusual for this working, survived until 25 February 1967. **Date: 13 May 1961.**

⬉ Lancaster shed (23C and 10J), in its last decade, gained a reputation for becoming a graveyard for classes before withdrawal. This was the case initially for the Midland Compounds, followed by the Hughes 'Crabs' and finally for the 'unrebuilt' 'Patriots', all of which were allocated and worked the passenger services to Leeds City and Bradford Forster Square. The shed closed in 1966, after being allocated codes 23C, 11E, 24J, and finally 10J, between 1950 and 1966. 'Crab' No 42928, in fine external condition, which had been allocated to Lancaster since May 1947, approaches Hellifield with an up express from Morecambe to Leeds. This 2-6-0 was withdrawn on 16 February 1963. **Date: 14 October 1961.**

⬅ Many locomotives around this period were in terrible external condition, and I often wonder why I bothered to take colour slides of them when black and white would have done just as well. Carlisle Kingmoor-allocated Stanier 8F No 48464, which had been at the shed since before 1950, is shown passing through Dent station with an up freight. Dent station, on the Settle & Carlisle line, is about halfway between Leeds and Carlisle and is the highest main line station in the country at 1,150ft. It opened on 6 August 1877 and closed on 4 May 1970, reopening again on 14 July 1986. It has a problem in that the villages it serves, namely Dent and Cowgill, are 600ft below the station, and some distance away. **Date: 13 May 1961.**

⬆ In the latter 1950s and early 1960s, Grantham shed seemed to suffer from a chronic shortage of cleaners, as shown in this picture of Class A3 No 60046 *Diamond Jubilee*, hauling the 11.37am Leeds Central to King's Cross. It has just passed the site of Holbeck High level station, which closed on 7 July 1958. The exit from Leeds Central involved a steep climb at 1 in 100/50 to Wortley South Junction, just past Copley Hill shed.

No 60046 entered service as an A3 on 23 August 1941 after having been modified from a Class A1. Its career as an A1 started on 9 August 1924. It was only ever allocated to sheds on the Eastern Region and was withdrawn on 16 June 1963. **Date: 28 August 1961.**

⬆ Rebuilt 'Royal Scots' were a familiar sight at Leeds City (Wellington Street) for 20 years and, from 1959 until around 1963, they were joined by rebuilt 'Patriots', which had been made redundant by the arrival of the diesels on the West Coast Main Line. No 45522 *Prestatyn*, which was allocated to Kentish Town shed (14B) at the time of this picture, is shown leaving Leeds City with the 12.35pm express to London St Pancras. Eighteen members of the class were rebuilt, No 45522 being the last in February 1949. It put in another 15 years of service before being withdrawn in September 1964, with a claimed mileage of 1,533,492 miles as at the end of 1960. **Date: 28 August 1961.**

⬆ Between June and August 1948, a small batch of Caprotti valve gear-fitted Class 5s, Nos 44743 to 44747, was allocated to Bristol Barrow Road (22A) shed, to work the expresses to Birmingham, York and Leeds. It was claimed they were slow in starting, but were strong and free steaming at speed. This bears out my limited experience, when travelling behind them in the early 1950s, as the climb out of Sheffield Midland to Totley seemed to take for ever, but the speed down the bank to Chesterfield and beyond was extremely fast.

They were eventually allocated away, as the 'Peak' class diesels took over, and in March 1962 they were allocated to Southport shed (27C) to work the Calder Valley expresses to Leeds and Bradford, as well as other services around Lancashire. This they did until the Calder Valley Class 110 DMUs took over the services in 1963, with Southport shed closing in 1966, then coded 8M. No 44744 is seen leaving Halifax on an evening train, which would have combined portions from Leeds and Bradford at the station. No 44744 was withdrawn on 23 November 1963. **Date: 6 July 1961.**

➡ Out of the 842 Class 5 4-6-0s, of various forms, No 44767 was unique. It emerged from Crewe Works in 1947, fitted with a double chimney, outside Stephenson link motion, and Timken roller bearings, which features it retained, except for the double chimney which it lost early on. By 1950, it was allocated to Bank Hall shed (27A) at Liverpool, where it remained until March 1962 so it could be seen frequently in Halifax where this picture was taken. It headed Calder Valley expresses between Liverpool Exchange, Bradford Exchange and Leeds Central.

After the Birmingham RCW Calder Valley DMUs (later Class 110s) took over in 1962, it was transferred to Southport shed and eventually to Carlisle Kingmoor in November 1964, where it stayed until withdrawn on 2 December 1967. It passed into preservation and has, over the years, worked many main line specials. From my occasional conversations with crews working the Calder Valley expresses, it was generally regarded as the best engine they had. Whether the double chimney made any difference, I don't think has ever really been established.

It is shown ready to leave Halifax station with an up evening express for Liverpool Exchange two months after the station name had officially been altered from Halifax Town to Halifax. **Date: 28 August 1961.**

1962

BRITISH RAILWAYS

From the steam enthusiasts' point of view, 1962 was a disaster. Everybody knew that sooner or later dieselisation and electrification would really hit the steam scene, and so it proved to be this year. Steam working finished in East Anglia from September resulting in the end of the following classes: J15, J17, J19, J20, J69 and N7, perhaps not exactly high-profile types but no doubt very much missed by those who lived in the area.

In Scotland, the most notable classes to vanish were the D11/2s with No 62685 *Malcolm Graeme* and, one of the best of all Scottish classes, the ex-North British Class D34 'Glens' with No 62496 *Glen Loy* being the last to go.

On the Western Region, the followers of 'God's Wonderful Railway' must have been devastated by the total elimination of the famous 'Kings', especially as earlier in the year, No 6011 *King James I* had received an overhaul at Swindon. Nos 6000, 6011, 6018 and 6025 were the last to be withdrawn.

Meanwhile, on the Southern Region, there were some notable last of classes to be withdrawn. Both the 'Schools' and the 'King Arthurs' became extinct and the Beattie well tanks ended their long association with the Wenford Bridge line, although by this time it was part of the Western Region.

On the London Midland, the end of the 'Princess Royals' was not a surprise, with the Fowler and Stanier 2-6-2Ts ending also. The much-maligned No 71000 *Duke of Gloucester* was withdrawn, and the WD 'Austerity' 2-10-0s became history. A sign of things to come was the withdrawal of some 'Princess Coronations' and half the BR Standard 6MT 'Clans' ended their very short careers. Overall, it was a depressing scene, which over the next few years would only get worse.

Lines which lost their passenger services included the following:

Taunton–Chard	Kingham–Chipping Norton
Gwinear Road–Helston	Newport–Ebbw Vale
Plymouth–Launceston	Barry–Pontypridd
Didcot–Newbury	Whitland–Cardigan
West Drayton–Uxbridge Vine Street	Wrexham–Ellesmere
Wellington, Buildwas and Much Wenlock	Neath–Brecon
Wolverhampton–Stourbridge Junction	Moat Lane–Three Cocks Junction
Bewdley–Tenbury Wells	Hereford–Brecon
Coaley Junction–Dursley	Newport–Brecon
Cheltenham–Kingham	Lugton–Beith

The list of classes and lines is probably incomplete, but it shows the extent to what was happening. If one looked hard, there was some good news. The four Scottish preserved locomotives were doing some excellent trips north of the border, and there were other memorable specials being run, usually to mark the end of a class of locomotive, or pending a line closure. The photographs in this section illustrate just a few of these events but, even if one could have devoted seven days a week throughout the year, one could hardly have managed to have kept pace with what was going on.

Another announcement of some significance was that 12 of the 29 workshops were to close during the following 12 months.

New diesel and electric classes were getting established, the most high profile being the Type 4 'Westerns' (later Class 52), while others appearing were the first 'Claytons' and the Ruston & Hornsby shunters for Southampton Docks. Also, there were the Southern's electro-diesels (later Class 73), but the real threat came from the first three Brush Type 4s (later Class 47) of which 512 would eventually be built. This class would decimate steam all over the country and 50 years later they are still the main power for excursion trains.

For me, it was probably the most hectic year in the UK; car mileage was astronomic, film consumption enormous, and time in the dark room ridiculous, but some memorable pictures were obtained.

Leeds Central station opened on 18 September 1848 and was eventually closed on 29 April 1967 when services were transferred to City station. Two Class J50 0-6-0Ts, Nos 68984 and 68988, were allocated to Copley Hill shed for moving coaches to and from Copley Hill sidings, about a mile from the station. No 68984 spent 23 years on these duties, while No 68988 managed 20 years. No 68984 is about to leave the station and tackle the 1-in-100 gradient to the sidings. **Date: 2 October 1962.**

↱ H.A. Ivatt designed Class J52 0-6-0ST of which No 1247 was built for the Great Northern Railway in 1899 by Sharp Stewart & Co, eventually becoming BR No 68846, ending its career at Hornsey shed in May 1959. It was painted in fully lined-out BR black livery, the only member of the class to be so treated. It was purchased for preservation by Captain Bill Smith and was kept at Mowlem's yard, just south of Hatfield, from where it ran several main line trips.

It arrived at the Keighley & Worth Valley Railway on 6 March 1965, being one of the first locomotives to be based at the line. It moved on to Tyseley's Standard Gauge Steam Trust and eventually became part of the NRM collection at York. It is seen at Ayot on the ex-Great Northern line between Hatfield and Dunstable, which was part of a Stephenson Locomotive Society 'Tour of Seven Branch Lines' special from Birmingham, where ex-LMS Fowler 2P 4-4-0 No 40646 was the main motive power. **Date: 14 April 1962.**

↗ As mentioned in the previous caption, the SLS Midland Area organised this 224-mile special with Fowler 2P 4-4-0 No 40646 as the main motive power. The route was as follows: Birmingham New Street–Nuneaton Abbey Junction–Trent Valley Curve–Coventry Loop–Northampton–Bedford–Hitchin–Langley Junction–Hertford–Welwyn Garden City–Hatfield–Leighton Buzzard–Weedon–Leamington Spa–Berkswell, and Birmingham New Street. If I remember correctly, the tour was over an hour late at one stage but, with some fine running and slack timing, arrived back at New Street virtually on time. No 40646 sparkles in the evening sunshine at Leighton Buzzard. **Date: 14 April 1962.**

→ One of the Dugald Drummond T9 class 4-4-0s (nicknamed 'Greyhounds'), No 120 (BR No 30120) is on Eastleigh shed, painted in London & South Western Railway apple green. It was withdrawn from Exmouth Junction at Exeter (72A) in 1961, but in March 1962 it was overhauled at Eastleigh Works and painted as shown. It was used on local services as well as working many specials. It was withdrawn again from service in October 1963 and stored at various locations until being exhibited at the Bluebell and the Mid Hants railways. Now part of the NRM collection it is at present on the Bodmin & Wenford Railway, in working condition.

The 66 examples of this class were built between 1899 and 1901, and with a few modifications, put in 60 years of excellent service, initially on LSWR expresses, and in later years on the lines west of Exeter. Thirteen of the class were converted for oil firing, but the experiment ended in 1948 and the locomotives involved were withdrawn. **Date: 22 April 1962.**

⬆ One of the trains that were used for running in locomotives after overhaul at Doncaster Works was the 10.10am from Leeds Central as far as Doncaster. Class A3 No 60066 *Merry Hampton* of King's Cross shed (34A) has just received what was to be its last general overhaul and is shown just south of Beeston Junction near Leeds heading for Wakefield Westgate. It was built as an A1, entering service at Haymarket shed on 16 July 1924.

It was converted to an A3 in December 1945 and after five years at Haymarket as an A3, it moved to the Eastern Region, where it stayed, sharing its time at the East Coast Main Line sheds, before finally being withdrawn on 8 September 1963 from 34A. **Date: 25 June 1962.**

↗ During part of April 1962, the 'White Rose' express from King's Cross to Leeds and Bradford carried this headboard, promoting the woollen industry in West Yorkshire. Two locomotives were specially cleaned for the trains: King's Cross Class A3 No 60107 *Royal Lancer*, and local Class B1 No 61024 *Addax*. *Royal Lancer* is ready to depart Leeds Central with the up train.

The Pullman coaches in the background are part of the 'Queen of Scots' train, heading for Glasgow Queen Street. The A3 entered service as A1 No 1476 on 26 May 1923. It was rebuilt as an A3 in October 1946 and was allocated to the main East Coast sheds of the Eastern Region, apart from two years at Leicester shed, on Great Central line services from June 1950 to July 1952. It was withdrawn from Grantham shed on 1 September 1963. **Date: 9 April 1962.**

→ This very lucky picture was taken from the cab of 'Deltic' No D9014, as we approached Wakefield Westgate station, showing Class A3 No 60107 *Royal Lancer* leaving with the Leeds portion of the down 'White Rose'. B1 class No 61024 *Addax* waits to back down to the station, to take over the Bradford portion. Both locomotives were carrying the 'Wool Wins' headboards. **Date: 7 April 1962.**

⬆ Here is another picture of the 10am Leeds Central to King's Cross, this time headed by Class A4 No 60030 *Golden Fleece*, which is working hard as it climbs the short, 1-in-50 gradient past Copley Hill shed, between Holbeck High Level and Wortley South Junction.

The Pacific entered service as No 4495 and was named *Great Snipe*, and in LNER green livery. Its livery was quickly altered to blue as it became one of the two engines to be allocated to the newly introduced 'West Riding Limited'. It was renamed *Golden Fleece* as this was considered more appropriate, as many of the passengers on the new, fast West Yorkshire to King's Cross express would be wool buyers attending London auctions. It spent its whole career allocated to the sheds at the southern end of the East Coast Main Line. Along with No 60014 *Silver Link*, it became the first of the class to be withdrawn on 29 December 1962, due to the arrival of the 'Deltics'. **Date: 9 April 1962.**

◤ Class A4 No 60006 *Sir Ralph Wedgwood* is shown passing Beeston Junction, on the outskirts of Leeds, heading the up 10am Leeds Central to King's Cross train. It entered service on 26 January 1938, numbered 4466 and named *Herring Gull*, which it carried until 1 December 1943, and was renamed on 6 January 1944. It spent 25 years allocated to King's Cross and Grantham sheds before moving to New England (35A) for four months. It was then transferred to Scotland, ending its career at Aberdeen Ferryhill (61B), working the Glasgow to Aberdeen expresses. It was withdrawn on 3 September 1965. Beeston Junction was where the line from Neville Hill and Hunslet used to join the main line. **Date: 6 June 1962.**

◄ For no logical reason, Class A4 No 60017 *Silver Fox* was one of my favourite members of the class. It was the last of the four silver A4s to enter service on 18 December 1935 as No 2512. Allocated to King's Cross shed, it remained there for its entire career of 28 years, except for the last four months, when at New England shed (35A). It did little work from there before being withdrawn on 29 October 1963.

It is seen leaving Doncaster one Sunday afternoon with an up express for King's Cross, and is in the customary immaculate external condition for 'Top Shed' at this period. In May 1957, while having a general overhaul, No 60017 became the first of the class to be fitted with a double chimney, except for the four which had had them fitted from new, 20 years earlier. **Date: 29 September 1962.**

A visit to Carmarthen shed (87G) fortunately coincided with 'Castle' class No 5054 *Earl of Ducie* being in the yard, three months after it had returned from Swindon Works following its last general overhaul, in June 1962. It was allocated here for two years, from 1960 to 1962, although it spent the majority of its career at Cardiff Canton, after entering service in June 1936 when named *Lamphey Castle*, these plates later being attached to No 7005.

No 5054 is recorded as having travelled 1,412,394 miles in service before being withdrawn on 24 October 1964. Its main claim to fame was that it was one of the three 'Castles' selected to haul the famous Ian Allan Great Western high-speed tour on 9 May 1964, from Paddington to Plymouth, returning via Bristol. Each locomotive was carefully selected as being in the best condition from those members of the class still in service.

It was allocated the Bristol–Paddington leg of the tour, the aim being to reach 100mph on the journey. As it turned out, the maximum speed reached was 96mph at Little Somerford, with the 100-minute schedule being reduced to 95 minutes 33 seconds.
Date: 9 September 1962.

This was the only occasion that I ever visited Fishguard Goodwick shed (87J). I only photographed two locomotives there; one being pannier No 9602 and the other was 'Modified Hall' No 6962 *Soughton Hall*, which was allocated to Old Oak Common (81A) for its entire career from 1944. It became the first of the class to be withdrawn, in 1963. Goodwick shed closed in 1963.
Date: 9 September 1962.

⬆ One of the impressive 7200 class 2-8-2Ts, No 7248, is seen on Swansea East Dock shed (87D), where it was allocated between October 1959 and December 1962, but having spent time at many different sheds during its career. There were 54 in the class, which were rebuilds of the 4200 and 5205 class 2-8-0Ts and they were introduced in 1934. Most of the class were at the South Wales sheds, and with a coal bunker capacity of five or six tons they were able to be used on longer distance mineral trains. No 7248 was withdrawn in 1965, being one of the last in service, with three surviving into preservation. **Date: 2 June 1962.**

⬇ Seventy of the 6100 class 2-6-2Ts were built between April 1931 and November 1935, primarily for working the suburban services out of Paddington, which they did until the introduction of DMUs. No 6132 is shown at its then home shed of Southall (81C), painted in unlined BR green livery. This was in keeping with the Western Region practice of having all passenger and mixed traffic locomotives in lined-green although, towards the end of steam, no lining was applied. Apart for one month at Severn Tunnel Junction shed (86E) in 1955, No 6132 was allocated to the 81-area sheds after Nationalisation and was withdrawn in September 1965. Southall shed closed in 1965. **Date: 14 October 1962.**

⬆ I was sitting in my car at Scout Green on Shap on yet another dull and miserable morning, having given the approaching train a casual glance in the distance, thinking it was just another dirty Class 5, when I realised it was a 'Princess Royal'. A very quick exit from the car ensued and a dash down the track to get this grab shot. It is hard to tell, but No 46208 *Princess Helena Victoria* is actually in red livery. The train was the 9.43am summer Saturdays Liverpool–Glasgow. As No 46208 was allocated to Edge Hill Liverpool (8A), it was covering for a failed English Electric Type 4 (Class 40) diesel. It was allocated to Edge Hill shed in September 1951 and was withdrawn on 31 December 1962, with a recorded mileage of 1,449,634. **Date: 30 June 1962.**

◤ This special must rank as probably the best I ever managed to photograph. It was blessed with perfect weather all day and stopped at most stations on the route, which was Glasgow to Oban via the West Highland line to Crianlarich Upper. It returned from Oban in the afternoon via Killin Junction and Callander. The timings were so easy and the traffic on the roads so light that I easily managed to take shots at more than 60 different locations in the day. If I remember correctly, there was only one other vehicle (a green Austin A35 van) following the train. How times have changed.

The Caledonian Single 4-2-2, No 123, and North British Railway 4-4-0 No 256 *Glen Douglas*, provided the very colourful motive power, and they performed well or, to be more accurate, *Glen Douglas* did the work and the Single looked after itself. It was very noticeable while the locomotives were on Oban shed that No 123 had all the attention and the 'Glen' was largely ignored by the shed staff. Obviously old rivalries still remained.

The special is seen leaving Oban at the start of the steep climb of 1 in 50 to the summit at Glencruitten, three miles away. **Date: 12 May 1962.**

◄ This is how photo stops used to be. Here, the passengers of the Caley 123 special had the opportunity to take pictures at Ardlui, while waiting for the arrival of a train from Fort William, headed by a Birmingham RCW Type 2 (Class 27) diesel. An eight-mile climb up Glenfinnan to the summit just before Crianlarich Upper was ahead for the crews, with the gradient as steep as 1 in 60 for most of the way, which was no trouble for the 'Glen', but hardly suitable for the 4-2-2. **Date: 12 May 1962.**

This is a general view taken in the ash pit area of the shed yard at York (50A). The picture has become more interesting over the years, as two of the locomotives featured have been preserved, namely Jubilee No 45690 *Leander*, allocated to Bristol Barrow Road at the time, and Class A4 No 60007 *Sir Nigel Gresley* of 'Top Shed' King's Cross (34A). They have since been frequent visitors to York and both have spent more time in preservation than they did in normal service. The other locomotive is Ivatt 4MT 2-6-0 No 43160, which was one of the members of the class to go new, to the ex-Midland & Great Northern shed at Melton Constable (32E). At the time of this picture it was at Colwick shed (40E), from where it was withdrawn on 9 January 1965. York shed closed in 1967 and became the NRM in 1975. **Date: 16 June 1962.**

The hard work for the fireman on Class V2 2-6-2 No 60950 would be over for a while, as it drifts out of Stoke Tunnel and starts to descend the gradient towards Grantham station, after the 18 miles of climbing from Helpston signalbox to Stoke Summit, the last 9 miles being at 1 in 200/170. No 60950 was built at Darlington and entered service on 26 June 1942, spending 21 years allocated to the shed at Doncaster (36A), until it was withdrawn on 22 September 1963. **Date: 7 July 1962.**

⬆ Another memorable visit to Shap was for all the wrong reasons, because the weather was so terrible. The back road from Kirkby Lonsdale to Low Gill was under at least two feet of water in places, with a local farmer doing very well out of charging to haul cars through with his tractor. The day produced four pictures, all of which were useless, except for this very fortunate flash of sun, just as 'Princess Coronation' No 46248 *City of Leeds* appeared through the woods at Thrimby Grange on the 2pm Glasgow–Manchester train. No doubt *City of Leeds* would have been taken off at Preston, as the Pacifics were seldom seen at Manchester Exchange and Victoria.

No 46248 was the last streamlined member of the class to be built, entering service on 2 October 1943, and sharing its time between Camden, Crewe North and Carlisle Upperby sheds. It was on the Crewe North allocation (5A) when it was withdrawn on 5 September 1964, with a total recorded mileage of 1,136,499. **Date: 11 August 1962.**

◥ The ex-Lancashire & Yorkshire Railway Class 27 0-6-0s, of which 365 were built at Horwich Works between October 1889 and January 1898, would have been a familiar sight around Sowerby Bridge for over 70 years. After being allocated all over the ex-L&Y system, No 52413, which was fitted with an extended smokebox, finally arrived at Sowerby Bridge shed (56E) in March 1962, six months before its withdrawal, having given 62 years of service. This picture was taken of it on the shed, which closed in 1964. **Date: 8 April 1962.**

◣ An excellent tour was run by the Halifax Railfans Club, starting at Sowerby Bridge and going to Doncaster, for a visit to the Plant (works) followed by a trip along the East Coast Main Line for another works visit at Darlington. Interesting motive power was provided in the form of ex-Lancashire & Yorkshire 0-6-0 A class No 52515 and ex-Midland 4F 0-6-0 No 44408. I believe the original request was for one of the last Ivatt J6 0-6-0s, No 64277, but apparently it was not considered fit for the journey.

This certainly did not apply to No 52515, as in the previous November it had arrived back at Low Moor shed, after an overhaul at Horwich Works, when everybody believed it had gone for scrapping. It was well known in the West Riding of Yorkshire, as it had been allocated to the local sheds since Nationalisation. Its last allocation was to Sowerby Bridge from where it was withdrawn on 17 November 1962, one year after its overhaul and having done virtually no work. It would have been an excellent candidate for preservation.

The empty stock for the special is seen coming off the siding, which used to form the track for the Rishworth Branch. It lost its passenger services in 1929 and closed to all traffic in 1953. **Date: 29 September 1962.**

⬆ The delightful Hayling Island branch opened on 17 July 1867 and eventually closed on 4 November 1963. It had a long association with the famous Stroudley 'Terrier' 0-6-0Ts, Class A1Xs. Here, No 32640 has arrived at North Hayling, about halfway along the branch, and is heading for Havant.

No 32640 was built as No 40 in 1878 and named *Brighton* by the London, Brighton & South Coast Railway. It had an interesting career, being sold to the Isle of Wight Central Railway in January 1902, when it became No 11 and later No W11 *Newport* under Southern Railway ownership. It was returned to the mainland in 1947 where it remained until withdrawn on 16 September 1963. It was rebuilt as an A1X in August 1918 from an A1.

Like many that survived to the 1960s, No 32640 was preserved, and has returned to the Isle of Wight Steam Railway. Not a bad investment for 85 years of service. **Date: 4 August 1962.**

⬅ The railways of the Isle of Wight, even as late as the early 1960s, were a hive of activity on summer Saturdays. Although the track mileage on the island had been reducing over the years, a stationmaster told me on one of my visits in 1961, that in the late 1950s they would carry 55,000 passengers on a summer Saturday. Sadly, the steam operation ended in 1966 with the section from Ryde to Shanklin being electrified, using ex-London Transport stock, which is still in operation today.

The services in BR days were operated almost entirely by the Class O2 0-4-4Ts, the first of which arrived on the island in 1925, with others following until as late as 1949. No 32, named *Bonchurch*, is shown leaving Ryde Pier Head after making a connection with a ferry from the mainland.

Fourteen of the 23 Class O2s, which were sent to the IOW, were still active during 1966, although No 32 was withdrawn in October 1964. During their time on the island they were painted in the various shades of Southern greens but ended up in BR lined-black livery, but No 24 *Calbourne* ran in unlined black at the end. It was withdrawn in March 1967 and fortunately passed into preservation on the Isle of Wight Steam Railway. In 2012, it was transported over to the mainland to run on various preserved lines, not having left the island since 1925.
Date: 2 August 1962.

↑ A joint tour was organised around south London by the RCTS and the SLS, using two of the famous Beattie 2-4-0WT well tanks, Nos 30585 and 30587. It was remarkable that after a gap of 60 years they should return to the London suburbs. The tour mileage was only 69½ but 56 were hauled by the 1874 Bayer Peacock veterans. The six-coach 210-ton load left Waterloo for Surbiton, where they are seen leaving for Hampton Court.

Not surprisingly, the 550-gallon capacity of the well tanks caused a problem, especially when the water supply at Hampton Court was frozen due to a severe overnight frost, needing the local fire brigade to come to the rescue. Fortunately, both locomotives have been preserved, No 30585 at the Buckingham Railway Centre and No 30587 at the Bodmin & Wenford Railway. **Date: 2 December 1962.**

→ Rather a lot of my time in 1962 was spent on specials, one of which was the Sussex Rail Tour from London Bridge. 'Schools' class 4-4-0 No 30925 *Cheltenham* was allocated a time of one hour to Brighton, but it took 64 minutes, due to permanent way workings.

At Brighton, 'Terrier' No 32636 took over with Class E6 0-6-2T No 32418, for a trip to Seaham via Lewes. The pair is seen inside Brighton station on the return, and this was probably the last occasion when two ex-London, Brighton & South Coast locomotives were seen in the station. The tour then returned to London headed by K class Mogul No 32353, via Horsham and Epsom. No 32636, which was originally LBSCR No 72 *Fenchurch*, is preserved on the Bluebell Railway, while No 32418 was withdrawn from Brighton shed on 17 December 1962. **Date: 7 October 1962.**

◁ It was an interesting start to the year in Mirfield in 1962, when the driver of Class V2 No 60954 thought he was on the main line but was actually on the loop. As can be seen, the catch points did their job perfectly and an excellent afternoon's entertainment was provided for the locals on the Sunday. Fortunately, the crew were unhurt and as the locomotive landed in soft earth there was little damage. No 60954 was sent to Darlington Works for a casual repair and continued in service at York shed, where it spent its entire career before being withdrawn on 18 November 1963. **Date: 7 January 1962.**

▷ The 'Queen of Scots' Pullman was introduced on 1 May 1928 and ran between King's Cross and Glasgow Queen Street via Leeds and Harrogate. It was reintroduced on 5 July 1948 after the war, with the last titled train running on 13 June 1964. In the early 1960s, the up train was a regular diagram for the Copley Hill (56C) Class A1s, and No 60145 *Saint Mungo* is seen heading such a train, past Beeston Junction to the south of Leeds. It was allocated to the shed in November 1960, which closed in 1964. No 60145 ended its 17-year career as a Darlington standby locomotive, from where it was withdrawn in March 1966, but it was reinstated and sent to York shed (50A), finally being withdrawn in June, making it the last member of the class in traffic. **Date: 7 June 1962.**

As usual, I had left it far too late to take photographs of Belah Viaduct, in fact, leaving it to the last day. The RCTS 'Stainmore Limited' headed by BR Standard 2-6-0s, 3MT No 77003 and 4MT No 76049 are seen crossing it on their way to Kirkby Stephen East. The viaduct was built in 1859 with a height above ground of 196ft and it was 1,047ft long. It was situated near Barras station up on the moors, and one had to pass through six farm gates on the narrow road to get near it. This section of the line opened on 4 July 1861, but the dismantling of the viaduct started very soon after the line closed.

Both engines were allocated to West Auckland shed (51F), which closed in 1964. No 77003 was withdrawn from Stourton shed (55B) on 3 December 1966 and No 76049 finished its career at Bathgate (64F) in Scotland, on 25 December 1965. **Date: 20 January 1962.**

⬆ The 'Castle' class must be regarded as one of the most successful express passenger locomotives to run in the UK. The first to appear was No 4073 *Caerphilly Castle* in 1923, followed by another 178 over a period of 37 years without any major modifications, until No 7018 *Drysllwyn Castle* was fitted with a double chimney in 1956.

The last to be built was No 7037 in August 1960, appropriately named *Swindon* and was supposed to be allocated to Worcester, but somehow it managed to remain at Swindon shed (82C) for ten years. It then moved to Old Oak Common (81A) in September 1960, from where it was withdrawn on 4 March 1963. It is shown on Neath shed (87A) on a visit, which was part of a hectic shed 'bash' to all the South Wales sheds in one weekend by car. **Date: 6 June 1962.**

◣ I was very fortunate to call at Westbury (82D) on this day to find 'King' class 4-6-0 No 6011 *King James I* on shed, fresh from an overhaul at Swindon Works. It seemed strange that an overhaul had been given by this late date, as there was very little work for the class, and withdrawals had already started. As it turned out, No 6011, along with Nos 6018 and 6025, became the last members of the class to be withdrawn, in December 1962. No 6011 entered service in April 1928 and received a double chimney in March 1956. It was allocated to Stafford Road shed (84A) Wolverhampton from at least 1950, except for its last three months of service. **Date: 25 February 1962.**

◀ This is a fine line-up of power at Carmarthen shed (87G). From left to right is 4900 class 4-6-0 No 5938 *Stanley Hall*, built July 1933 and withdrawn 4 May 1963. Alongside it to the right is 'Castle' No 4081 *Warwick Castle*, built 1924 and giving 39 years of service, ending on 1 January 1963 with a recorded mileage of 1,897,998. Finally another 'Castle' class No 5087 *Tintern Abbey*, built in 1940 and withdrawn on 27 July 1963. Carmarthen shed closed in 1964. **Date: 9 September 1962.**

I have already mentioned on page 54 how the Leeds–Lancaster Morecambe services, in the last years of steam, were often worked by the last examples of ex-LMS classes. By this date it was the turn of the 'unrebuilt' 'Patriots' to be used, as seen here with No 45550 passing Bingley, with the Bradford portion of the evening Morecambe Residential, which combined with a Leeds portion at Skipton.

The other members of the class working the service were in poor condition, but No 45550 had had a visit to Crewe Works as late as November 1961. Its recorded mileage at the end of 1960 was 1,213,962, and it was placed in store at Preston shed in September 1962. It was still being present in July 1963 but was scrapped at Crewe Works in August. Fifty-two 'Patriots' were built between 1930 and May 1934, 18 being rebuilt to be almost identical to the rebuilt 'Royal Scots', with No 45550 being the last of the 'unrebuilt' ones to survive. **Date: 10 May 1962.**

The Swanage branch opened on 20 May 1885 and survived until 3 January 1972, when BR closed it and lifted the track. In 1975, volunteers started the long process of relaying, culminating with the first through, 12-coach special being run from Waterloo to Swanage on 1 April 2009. The line has now become one of the country's main preserved railways. Back in the Southern and BR days, the services were dominated by the famous Dugald Drummond M7 class 0-4-4Ts until Ivatt 2MT 2-6-2Ts appeared in the mid-1960s. DMUs then took over until closure.

M7 No 30057, allocated to Bournemouth shed (71B) since 1956, and a regular performer on the line, is seen leaving on a push-pull train from Swanage for Wareham. The class entered service in 1897 with 105 being built and the last one was withdrawn in May 1964. Two examples have been preserved, with No 30053 currently based at Swanage. **Date: 27 October 1962.**

Here is another view of Swanage station, taken four months before the previous picture. This time, it is M7 No 30111 working the service, which was allocated to Bournemouth shed (71B) by 1950. It remained there until withdrawn on 7 January 1963, so it must have travelled thousands of miles on the branch. **Date: 9 June 1962.**

⬆ The local enthusiasts had little time to accumulate a collection of pictures of the unrebuilt 'Patriots' working the Leeds-Morecambe trains, as in some cases, they were only about for a few months. No 45550 is seen again on the same train as in the previous picture, but this time shutting off steam, on the approach to Thwaites on the outskirts of Keighley.
Date: 16 May 1962.

⬆ One of the 90 6400/7400 class 0-6-0PTs, designed by Collett and built between 1932 and 1950, is at Merthyr station in full BR lined-green livery, ready to leave on the auto train service to Hirwaun. The train did not actually depart, as a furious argument broke out between the fireman and the driver, resulting in the fireman hurling his shovel at the driver and storming off down the platform. No 6416 survived until 1 September 1963, which was probably considerably longer than the fireman did in BR employment. **Date: 10 September 1962.**

↥ It is hard to believe that three months after this picture was taken, Brecon would completely lose its connection to the national rail network, which it had enjoyed since 1871, thus becoming the first county in England and Wales to be without a railway service. Pannier tank No 9631, which continued in service until 13 June 1965, has just been turned on the small turntable. Class 2251 No 3201, as detailed previously, waits to leave with a train to Merthyr and Newport, which will climb the steep gradient past Talybont-on-Usk to the summit at Torpantu. **Date: 10 September 1962.**

↖ Talyllyn Junction was a delightful country station, where the ex-Cambrian Mid-Wales line joined the ex-Brecon & Merthyr line. The station opened on 1 October 1869 and closed on 31 December 1962. Collett 2251 class 0-6-0 No 3201, which was working a Brecon to Merthyr and Newport service, is waiting for the arrival of a Mid-Wales line train. A total of 125 of the class were built between 1930 and 1948; No 3201 entered service in 1946, lasting 19 years before withdrawal on 15 May 1965. **Date: 10 September 1962.**

← The Ivatt 2MT 2-6-0s were the main motive power for the local Cambrian services at the end of steam. No 46521, in full BR lined-green livery is seen arriving at Talyllyn Junction, with the Mid-Wales service mentioned in the previous caption, and was heading for Brecon, only a few miles away. Passenger services ceased on the Mid-Wales line from Moat Lane Junction on 31 December 1962. **Date: 10 September 1962.**

1963

This was a far less active year for me than 1962, although I did travel and photograph several railtours. Some of these are illustrated here, but the railway scene as a whole was far from quiet. The Beeching report on 'Reshaping the Railways' appeared on 27 March 1963, the most important report ever to be produced on the railways. The contents were stark, saying the future of the railways would change for ever. Studying the detail from an enthusiast's point of view it appeared the world was ending, but the hard truth was, in the 1960s, the public were flocking to cars and the majority of the rail network was a financial disaster.

In broad outline, the savings were to be £85 million per year; I have seen other figures quoted, which would eventually involve the closure of about half the network. It was claimed that the elimination of steam would save £20 million per annum, and while the other figures that went up to produce this impressive savings total looked fine, the consequences of the thousands of job losses seemed to be overlooked. Even by 1963, only 23 per cent of passenger services were steam hauled, which had resulted in the elimination of many steam classes. Some of these classes are listed below:

Southern Region E2, E4, B4, A1X (Terriers)   Eastern Region O2/2, J50
Western Region 5400, 1500   Scottish Region Pickersgill 3F

Other 'lasts' were the South Tyneside electrics and diesel-electrics Nos 10201, 10202 and 10203. Notable withdrawals were A3 No 60103 *Flying Scotsman* in January, with a last high-profile publicity trip, but it was back on the main line in preservation by April. *Mallard*'s career also came to an end.

There was some good news on the narrow gauge with the Welshpool & Llanfair running its first services in preservation, and a Royal Train was run in the Isle of Man for the first time. Another news worthy event was the 'Great Train Robbery' at Sears Crossing, which over the years has received so much publicity.

Notable line closures included the following:

Chasewater–Newquay   Havant–Hayling Island
Churston–Brixham   Woodall Junction–Boston
Witham–Yatton via Cheddar   Goxhill–Immingham Dock
Tiverton Junction–Hemyock   Pinxton (South)–Kimberley (East)
Brent–Kingsbridge   Cresswell–Cheadle
Exeter–Dulverton via Tiverton   Ashchurch–Redditch
Seven Sisters via Palace Gates   Bewdley–Shrewsbury
Oxford–Princess Risborough   Wellington–Market Drayton
Radley–Abingdon   Llandeilo–Carmarthen
Haywards Heath–Horsted Keynes   Tondu–Pyle

While the closure of these lines must have been a blow to the local communities at the time, I doubt if the retention of any of these really could have been justified financially, but it is interesting to see the list includes the former main line connection with the Bluebell Railway from Horsted Keynes and what was to become the Severn Valley Railway on part of the Bewdley to Shrewsbury line.

Other items of note during the year were the opening of Millerhill marshalling yard, the introduction of the Mk2 coach, the London Underground Centenary celebrations on 23 May, and the prototype 'Deltic' being retired from service. Closer to my home area was the closure of the Settle & Carlisle line in January by snow, for several days. The first Brush Type 4 diesel-electric (later Class 47) was seen in Leeds, and I recorded my highest speed on the footplate of a steam locomotive at 94mph.

⬆ The snow fences at Dent had not done a good job during the heavy snow in January 1963, when the line was closed for around a week. Apparently, it had reopened earlier in the day and was extremely busy with freight and I decided to drive to Dent, after filling the boot of my VW Beetle (which is at the front of course), with heavy scrap metal to give it some weight. By some miracle, I managed to climb the very steep hill from the bottom of Dentdale to the station.

Dent is the highest main line station in England at 1,145ft and was opened in August 1877. Unfortunately, it is four miles from the community it is supposed to serve, which is 600ft lower. It is also halfway between Leeds and Carlisle. Carlisle Kingmoor Class 5 No 44669 is passing through the station on a down freight, and the depth of the snow can be seen on the up side with Wold Fell providing the backdrop. It was said the conditions were not nearly as bad as in 1947, when the line was closed for around four weeks. The 'Black Five' was a Carlisle Kingmoor locomotive for its entire career, which ended on 7 October 1967. **Date: 26 January 1963.**

↑ This is the plaque carried by Class A4 No 60022 *Mallard* to commemorate its world speed record of 126mph. At the time of the record it was No 4468.
Date: 17 June 1962.

↑ As I had made such an effort to get to Dent in these conditions, I thought I could include one more snow picture. It is another Carlisle Kingmoor Class 5, this time No 45491 heading a down freight approaching the station. It would be a long time before all the snow cleared from the up platform. No 45491 was allocated to Kingmoor in July 1952 and remained there until withdrawn on 19 June 1965. It later passed into preservation, but as yet, has not been returned to working order.
Date: 26 January 1963.

↗ This sorry sight greeted me on a visit to Doncaster Works in March. No 60014 *Silver Link* and No 60030 *Golden Fleece* had become the first of the famous Class A4s to be withdrawn, on 29 December 1962. It was rumoured that Silver Link was available for sale for £3,000 but unfortunately there were no takers. This locomotive really should have been preserved after its incredible achievements in the early days of the 'Silver Jubilee', rather than the less-famous examples which reached preservation later, with the exception of *Mallard*, but that was a lot of money in 1963. **Date: 3 March 1963.**

→ Time was rapidly running out even for No 60022 *Mallard* as it only had another month in service when this picture was taken, but it was looking in good external condition. One week earlier, it had worked a special from Waterloo to Exeter Central and then to Westbury. It must have still been in good mechanical order, as it achieved 90mph four times during that trip. It entered service on 3 March 1938 and was one of the four members of the class that had the double chimney fitted from new. It was initially allocated to Doncaster shed (36A) and then moved to Grantham (35B) in October 1943, before moving to 'Top Shed' (King's Cross 34A) in April 1948, with which it has always been associated. It is seen on the turntable at Doncaster shed. Withdrawal came on 25 April 1963. **Date: 3 March 1963.**

↑ Two different types of Pacifics are seen alongside each other under the coaler at Carlisle Kingmoor shed. On the left is BR Standard 6MT 'Clan' No 72009 *Clan Stewart*, which spent its entire, short working career of just over 13 years allocated to the shed, except for two months in 1958, when it was sent to Stratford shed (30A) in London, for trials on the ex-Great Eastern services. Withdrawal came on 28 August 1965. 'Princess Coronation' No 46226 *Duchess of Norfolk* in red livery, was also allocated to Kingmoor as from March 1961, and remained until withdrawn on 12 September 1964, with a recorded mileage of 1,456,949 over 26 years. The shed closed in 1968 and during the 1950s had an allocation of just over 140 locomotives. When passing in the train today, the site is virtually a forest, part of which is now a wildlife reserve. **Date: 6 April 1963.**

↖ ← Here, two 'Princess Coronations' in different liveries, face each other in Carlisle Kingmoor shed. On the left is No 46242 *City of Glasgow* in green livery and on the right, No 46247 *City of Liverpool* in red. No 46242 was one of the locomotives involved in the terrible Harrow crash on 8 October 1952. It received extensive repairs over 291 days, re-entering service on 26 October 1953. It was originally a streamlined locomotive but when it reappeared after the crash overhaul, the front end had been repaired with the draping curve in front of the cylinders, a feature previously only applied to the non-streamlined examples of the class. The difference can be clearly seen compared with No 46247, which by this date had only another seven weeks to go before withdrawal. No 46242 lasted a little longer, until 19 October 1963. Records show that No 46247 achieved 1,388,197 miles in its 20-year career, while No 46242 managed 1,555,280 in 22 years. **Date: 6 April 1963.**

⬆ This was a joint tour organised by the Stephenson Locomotive Society and the Railway Correspondence & Travel Society, which gave a rare opportunity to travel over the Settle & Carlisle line behind a 'Princess Coronation', although the RCTS had had No 46247 *City of Liverpool* over the line in 1961. No 46238 *City of Carlisle* was the allocated locomotive but, with only five coaches in tow, I gather it was rather an unexciting trip to Carlisle compared with outings behind *City of Liverpool*, and the preserved *Duchess of Hamilton* and *Duchess of Sutherland*. The picture was taken by the signalbox at Dent on a fine day, when Wold Fell and Arten Gill Viaduct stood out clearly. No 46238 had been allocated to Carlisle Upperby shed (12B) since September 1951, and was withdrawn on 12 September 1964 with 1,602,628 miles recorded in 25 years. **Date: 27 September 1963.**

⬆ The nameplate of ex-Great Western 'King' class No 6018 *King Henry VI*. **Date: 17 December 1962.**

⬇ As already mentioned on page 80, all the famous ex-Great Western 'King' class had been withdrawn by the end of 1962. The Stephenson Locomotive Society in the Birmingham area obviously had connections in the Western Region hierarchy, as special permission was given to have No 6018 *King Henry VI* reinstated for a very last 'King Farewell' trip, on 28 April 1963, after which it returned to store at Swindon. The locomotive was prepared for the trip by Tyseley shed (84E) and they removed the front number plate and painted TYS on the front frame, in old Great Western style.

   The route of the tour was from Birmingham Snow Hill to Southall, continuing to Swindon for a works and shed visit, where the special actually ran into the works area, before returning to Birmingham. The loco was obviously in good condition, reaching 90mph down the bank before High Wycombe, with the climb from Warwick up Hatton bank being outstanding. The 'King' was positioned on the shed, where hundreds of other locomotives had been photographed over the years. Also on shed was No 4079 *Pendennis Castle*, which was withdrawn in May 1964, before being preserved. **Date: 28 April 1963.**

Inside one of the roundhouses at Leeds Holbeck shed (55A) is 'Jubilee' class No 45639 *Raleigh*, which had been on the shed allocation since July 1951. It entered service in December 1934 and worked from the main line ex-Midland main sheds, until arriving at Holbeck. Up to 1950 it had accumulated 888,512 miles. During the 1950s, Holbeck had between 18 and 20 'Jubilees' on its allocation, out of a total of 80 to 90 locomotives. Mileage records show that the Holbeck 'Jubilees' consistently recorded the highest miles per annum for the class, which is no surprise, as their regular diagrams included Leeds to Glasgow, London and Bristol. **Date: 15 September 1963.**

Here is another view inside the very atmospheric Leeds Holbeck roundhouses. This time, 'Jubilee' No 45647 *Sturdee* is shown. It was on the Saltley (21A) allocation at the time of this picture, but was transferred to Holbeck shed in November 1966. Before that, it had nearly always been at sheds associated with West Coast Main Line services. It was on the allocation for six months before it was withdrawn in April/May 1967, but had run 1,293,844 miles according to the records up to 1960, having entered service in October 1935. **Date: 23 September 1963.**

↑ Back in 1963, 'Britannias' were not a common sight on the Calder Valley main line. It was a surprise when No 70039 *Sir Christopher Wren* turned up on a Scunthorpe–Blackpool Illuminations special, which is seen passing Sowerby Bridge. Had the exhaust not obscured it, the skyline would have shown a famous local landmark named Wainhouse Tower, which at 275ft is the highest folly in the world, built between 1871 and 1875. After just over seven years working the expresses out of Liverpool Street, No 70039 moved to Immingham shed (40B) for three years, where it was allocated when this picture was taken. It moved to Carlisle in 1963 like most of the class, from where it was withdrawn on 9 May 1967. **Date: 8 September 1963.**

↑ Details about the Gresley Class K4 2-6-0s have already been given on page 25. No 3442 (BR No 61994) was withdrawn in December 1961 from Thornton Junction shed (62A), but was purchased by the late Viscount Garnock and was restored to working order at Cowlairs Works, Glasgow. In April, it worked south on a special goods train to Neville Hill shed (50B), which became its base for the next nine years. During this period, it worked several specials on the main lines but in this picture it is working an inspection special and is seen at Wetherby East during a lunch break. This line from Church Fenton to Wetherby closed to all traffic on 30 November 1966. It is currently running as No 61994 *The Great Marquess* and is very active working on Network Rail. **Date: 25 September 1963.**

↗ Later in the day, the inspection special was shunted into the siding at Pannal station on the Leeds–Harrogate line, to let a service train pass. **Date: 25 September 1963.**

→ The first tour that *The Great Marquess* undertook in preservation was the RCTS 'Dalesman', which passed Otley and Ilkley en route to Skipton, followed by trip up the Grassington branch. It then headed for East Lancashire, where it is seen passing Earby station on the Skipton to Colne line, which closed on 2 February 1970. There have been many serious attempts in recent years to get the line reopened, which are still on going.
    The unfamiliarity of the crews with the type of locomotive, and the fact it was badly 'off beat', resulted in a very late arrival back in Leeds. **Date: 4 May 1963.**

↑ My friend, Bill Anderson, was good enough to take me to this fine location at Achalader, just north of Bridge of Orchy, where we photographed *Glen Douglas* and J37 No 64632 heading north. At this point, he lost interest in the train and went for a swim in Loch Tulla, seen in the background. This was before the days when every sleeper length of the line was known by enthusiasts and 'photters'. No 64632 continued in service until 1 December 1965. **Date: 1 June 1963.**

↖ The 'Jacobite' special was advertised as definitely the last steam passenger train over the West Highland line. It was blessed with perfect weather and was certainly one of the most interesting tours I have ever followed. The day started badly though, by falling out with the landlady in Helensburgh, when we asked for an early breakfast as we had a train to catch. We were told that there was not a train at that time on the railway so we did not need an early start!

We duly arrived at Garelochhead to meet the special, which we then followed, obtaining plenty of good pictures as far as Tyndrum Upper. At this point my trusty Volkswagen Beetle refused to restart. The signalman, noticing our troubles, shouted that he would come and fix it, which he did after I pointed out to him that the engine was at the rear and not at the front. There were no further car problems during the day and it hardly cost us a picture. We drove to Tulloch to be faced with a long wait, as the ex-North British Railway Class J37, No 64632 had expired at Rannoch, having run hot. When the train appeared, we had the very rare sight of a North British Type 2 diesel rescuing 4-4-0 *Glen Douglas* (which had also failed, having dropped some of its firebars), rather than one of the diesels being rescued as was usual with that class. The train continued to Mallaig behind two more Class J37s, Nos 64592 and 64636, where it is seen heading towards Glenfinnan. **Date: 1 June 1963.**

← This was a carefully chosen location near Corpach to show Ben Nevis in the background, but the exhaust spoilt it. At this stage all was well with the locomotives but later, J37 No 64592 I am told, started to run hot, so when the special eventually reached Mallaig very late, it was decided to return to Glasgow behind a Birmingham RCW Type 2 (Class 27) diesel, which arrived at Glasgow Queen Street well after midnight. With three out of four locomotives failing on one trip, (is this a record?), I am sure that those at Scottish Region headquarters in Glasgow definitely meant it to be the last steam trip on the West Highland line. How wrong could they have been! **Date: 1 June 1963.**

1964

The year was dominated by the number of line and passenger service closures, which I estimate at around 62, leaving many areas of the UK completely without any railways. The Beeching axe was really being felt and trying to keep up with them was a losing battle. On certain days, such as 7 September, no fewer than ten services ended.

There was also bad news on the locomotive front, but by far the worst for most enthusiasts was the withdrawal of the remaining 'Princess Coronations'. This was not because of their mechanical condition in many cases, but because there was no longer any suitable work for them. Other important classes which became extinct on the network were the GWR 4700 2-8-0s, the famous Somerset & Dorset 2-8-0s, and the last of the once 935 members of the LMS 3F 0-6-0s. Others of note lost, were the Southern M7 class 0-4-4Ts, the LNER B16/2 4-6-0s, and the LMS dock tanks.

Events of note were the last run with steam of the 'Atlantic Coast Express', after 38 years, and diesels taking over the Lickey banking duties. A first for me was an invitation to travel on a private charter with Class K4 No 3442 *The Great Marquess*, from Leeds to Whitby over the North Yorkshire Moors, although I chose to photograph the train by car for most of the trip.

No 4472 *Flying Scotsman* was hauled, while in steam, through the New Woodhead Tunnel by an electric loco, which was probably the first time this had happened. My highlight of the year, however, was being on the footplate of 'Merchant Navy' No 35012 *United States Line* on the RCTS 'Solway Ranger' special over the Settle & Carlisle. I think I can now tell this story, as those involved are sadly no longer around. The Leeds Holbeck pilotman did not know there was no water scoop on the MN and the driver thought he would be told where to stop for water. We arrived at Settle Junction with the tender virtually dry and only by some very careful handling did we get to Hellifield. I have never seen a crew get the water column bag into a tender so quickly!

This will be remembered in West Yorkshire as the year when it was visited by probably the two most unlikely classes of locomotives since the war. The first was the Highland 4-6-0 'Jones Goods', as illustrated on page 113 at Holbeck shed Leeds, and the other was an ex- Great Western 'Grange' class 4-6-0, No 6858 *Woolston Grange*, when working a cross-country service and was not removed from the train at either Leicester or Nottingham. It got to Sheffield Victoria, where there was no other locomotive waiting to take over, so the driver carried on, unaware that the class was out of gauge for the route to Huddersfield, resulting in it hitting a platform edge between Penistone and Huddersfield.

The number of closures is too many to list in their entirety, so included here are just a few of the most important, although no doubt the importance depended on where you lived in the UK:

Broadstone–Brockenhurst 4 May
Sheringham–Melton Constable 6 April
Etruria–Kidsgrove 2 March
Kemble–Cirencester–Tetbury 6 April
Northampton–Wellingborough 4 May
Worcester–Bromyard 7 September
Leicester–Burton-on-Trent 7 September
Derby Friargate–Nottingham 7 September
Gloucester–Hereford 1 November
Pontypool–Neath 15 June

Bridgend–Barry 15 June
Carmarthen–Aberystwyth 14 December
Cross Gates–Wetherby 6 January
Bishop Auckland–Durham and Sunderland 4 May
Preston–Southport 6 September
Hull–Hornsea and Withensea 19 October
Ayr–Dalmellington 6 April
St Boswells–Berwick-on-Tweed 15 June
Gleneagles–Comrie 6 June
Plus about 42 more.

Looking to the future and the continuance of the railways on a positive note, the first 'Merry Go Round' power station coal trains were introduced, as well as the 'Cartic' trains. These took cars from the manufacturers directly to the docks for export, while the first of the Mk2 coaches were introduced as set XP 64 and put to work on the 'Talisman' express between London King's Cross and Edinburgh.

I only managed to visit the Tyne Dock–Consett line on one occasion, much to my regret. This picture shows BR Standard 9F No 92066 under the massive iron ore bunkers at Tyne Dock. The line had to climb 900ft in a matter of 23 miles, involving gradients in places of around 1 in 40 and 1 in 50. The 2-10-0 9Fs, of which ten were modified with Westinghouse air compressors, Nos 92060–66 and 92097–99, were dedicated to the workings, taking up their duties in 1956. Before that the trains were worked by Class Q7 0-8-0s and O2 2-8-0s for several years.

The minimum service involved ten locomotives for ten trains per day, but after 1954 this could be increased to 14, the journey time being 1 hour 51 minutes up the hill, and 1 hour 11 minutes down. There were ten bunkers capable of holding 750–1,250 tons of ore each and below these was a further set of mobile bunkers, which could receive weighed loads from those above and, if necessary, blend the ore before loading it into the train. Diesels eventually took over, with the last steam working on 19 November 1966, hauled by a suitably cleaned No 92063. The 9Fs were then stored, except for No 92065, which moved to Wakefield shed (56A), with No 92066 being withdrawn on 23 May 1965. **Date: 18 March 1964.**

↑ Here is a view taken inside one of the roundhouses at Leeds Neville Hill shed (then coded 55H), of Class Q6 0-8-0 No 63348 and A1 Pacific No 60134 *Foxhunter*, both then allocated to the shed, although the Q6 was withdrawn two weeks later with Foxhunter lasting until 23 May 1965. Originally, the shed had four large roundhouses, but in 1958 two were demolished and the remaining ones re-roofed. In 1950, it had an allocation of 81, which by 1959 had dropped to 54. The shed closed to steam in 1966 and became a diesel depot, and is still very much in use today. **Date: 10 May 1964.**

← This group of local Class Q6s, lined up in what remained of the roundhouse at Tyne Dock shed (52H) they are Nos 63371, 63393 and 63411. The 0-8-0s had been the mainstay of the freight operations in the North East since 1913, together with the J27 0-6-0s and lasted until steam finished in the area in 1967. The shed had an allocation in 1950 of 48, and nine years later, had only reduced to 44, dropping to 25 in 1965. The shed closed on 9 September 1967. **Date: 18 March 1964.**

⬆ Aberystwyth was a sub-shed to Machynlleth (89C). It had the reputation in the 1950s and early 1960s of keeping the 'Manor' class locomotives allocated to it in immaculate condition, for working the 'Cambrian Coast Express'. No 7803 *Barcote Manor* is seen on the shed being serviced after working the down train. Sadly, after the London Midland Region took over the area in 1963 and replaced the ex-Great Western locomotives with BR Standards, cleaning became something of the past, until the final days of steam, when an occasional engine received attention from enthusiasts. The shed closed in 1966, but *Barcote Manor* was withdrawn on 27 March 1965 after 27 years of service. **Date: 30 May 1964.**

⬆ *Barcote Manor* nameplate. **Date: 30 May 1964.**

⬆ The 'County' class was really the final development of Churchward's 'Saints', which had appeared 43 years earlier. Thirty examples were built between 1945 and 1947, which were roughly as powerful as the 'Castle' class, but they had route and speed restrictions initially imposed upon them due to the weight carried on the coupled wheels, which greatly increased hammer blow on the track. The first example, No 1000, had a double chimney, but the rest were built with single ones. They had a reputation for being poor steamers and suffered from a surging motion. Hawksworth, who designed them, decided in 1956 to fit them with a new double-blastpipe after extensive trials, which did improve the steaming (if not the looks) of the class. No 1013 *County of Dorset* is on Swindon shed (82C) in clean condition, although it was withdrawn three months later with the class becoming extinct during the year. **Date: 26 April 1964.**

⬅ This is another picture on Swindon shed during a visit that was part of a tour, which had started at Hereford and was hauled by 'Castle' No 4079 *Pendennis Castle*. Fortunately, No 7029 *Clun Castle* had been well positioned for photography in the yard. Both locomotives are preserved with No 7029 hauling many main line trips. No 4079 went to Australia, from where it has returned and is now at the Didcot Railway Centre. At the moment, neither is in main line running order, being under overhaul, but will no doubt appear on the network again in the future. **Date: 26 April 1964.**

↑ 'Princess Coronation' No 46225 *Duchess of Gloucester* makes a fine sight in the afternoon sun outside Carlisle Upperby shed, where it was allocated at the time of the photograph. It was the first of the class to receive the maroon and gold-striped livery when it was streamlined in May 1938, but the casing was removed in March 1947. It was allocated to the main English west coast sheds for virtually all its career, although it is recorded that it spent six months on the Holyhead allocation, between October 1939 and April 1940. It became one of the last to be withdrawn, on 12 September 1964. **Date: 18 March 1964.**

↑ No 6229 (46229) *Duchess of Hamilton* was built at Crewe in September 1938, but was renumbered and renamed 6220 *Coronation* for the trip to America in 1939, eventually returning to traffic in March 1942 and receiving its proper identity in April 1943. It was de-streamlined in December 1947 and remained in BR service until being withdrawn on 15 February 1964, after 26 years. Its second career then started when, along with classmate No 6233 (46233) *Duchess of Sutherland*, it was purchased by Sir Billy Butlin, for display at his holiday camps. It duly entered Crewe Works for a cosmetic restoration and emerged, as seen here, on Crewe North shed (5A) awaiting transfer to Minehead, where it remained until 1976. It was then placed on loan to the NRM on a 20-year agreement, but was purchased in 1987. Prior to then, it had been running specials on the main lines until 1985. It was overhauled and returned to active service from 1989 to 1996. It then went on static display at the NRM.

A decision was taken to have it re-streamlined, the contract being awarded to Tyseley Locomotive Works, which did a superb job for all now to see in the museum. There have been talks about it being returned to main line service, but as yet nothing has happened. As and when it does, I hope I am around to see it. **Date: 18 April 1964.**

↑ ← Here are two further pictures taken at the Staveley Works, but this time featuring one of the Kitson of Leeds 0F 0-4-0STs. There were ten in the class, built in two batches 23 years apart. The first batch of five appeared in 1932 and were built in Leeds, while the final five were constructed at Horwich Works in 1955. There were differences; the latter batch having shorter saddle tanks and extra space for coal bunkers. They were used on the Cromford & High Peak Railway, but Nos 47001 and 47005 were allocated to Staveley shed (41H) in October 1965. When the shed closed they moved to Barrow Hill, where they both remained until withdrawn on 3 December 1966. No 47005 is shunting around the works and appears to have recently visited Derby Works for overhaul. **Date: 9 May 1964.**

◥ The Staveley Iron & Steel Co, not far from Chesterfield, used to hire in locomotives from BR to operate their internal railway system, rather than having their own shunters. Apparently, the only locomotives suitable for the work were ex-Midland 0-6-0Ts, designed by Johnson in 1880, of which 240 were built, although only 95 passed into BR ownership. There was a small number retained in service at Staveley Barrow Hill to fulfil this contract, resulting in them remaining in service for far longer than BR probably wanted, in fact, to early 1964. No 41708 was one of the locomotives and, when withdrawn, was bought for preservation and sent to the Keighley & Worth Valley Railway.

It had a rather protracted journey to Haworth, after it ran hot en route and spent some time at Leeds Holbeck shed, where it could be seen with all its wheels out, mounted on sleepers. It worked on the Worth Valley for a short time before moving on to pastures new. **Date: 9 May 1964.**

⬆ This was a three-day special organised jointly by the Branch Line Society, the SLS Scottish area, and the Scottish Locomotive Preservation Fund. The attraction for me was that one of my favourite Pacifics, the Class A2s, would be working the train from Glasgow Queen Street to Aberdeen, No 60527 *Sun Chariot* being the chosen locomotive. The weather was poor and, after seeing it climb Cowlairs bank with a light load, I headed for Dundee. Here, the A2 handed over to a Class J37 for a trip on the lines to Auchterhouse and Kingsmuir, before arriving at Broughty Ferry, where the A2 took over again. The picture shows it at Broughty Ferry before I decided to follow to Aberdeen.

There was an important Scottish football fixture on this day, resulting in the roads being empty, but I never managed to get far enough in front of the train to get another picture and arrived at Aberdeen station virtually at the same time as the train. The special returned to Glasgow ready for the following day, to travel on lines around Lesmahagow, Carstairs, Wilsontown, Broughton and Moffat. The tour continued on the Monday, but I had to return home. By this date, No 60527 was one of the A2s allocated to Polmadie (66A), where they had been sent to replace the 'Princess Coronations' and, I am told, did not exactly please the Polmadie crews. No 60527 was withdrawn on 27 February 1965 having done little work during its two years at Polmadie. **Date: 28 March 1964.**

↑ The 'Jubilee Requiem' tour ran on 24 October 1964 as a final farewell to steam out of King's Cross, although regular steam working had already finished. It was organised jointly by the SLS and RCTS and ran to Newcastle and return. It would have been nice to have had one of the famous King's Cross A4s haul the train, but No 60009 *Union of South Africa* was in the best condition, being the last of the class to be overhauled at Doncaster, and was therefore chosen. It was very well turned out and is seen being serviced on Gateshead shed (52A), ready for the return trip. It was intended to achieve 100mph down Stoke bank and it was reported this was registering on the speedometer passing Essendine North signalbox. This was a fantastic performance, as the special only passed Stoke Summit at 57mph, but the time recorders on the train said it averaged more than 95mph between Little Bytham and Essendine, a distance of 3.8 miles, so it is probable the magic 'Ton' was achieved.

No 60009 was one of Haymarket's favourite A4s and was allocated from new to the shed, until being transferred to Aberdeen Ferryhill for its last four years, to work the three-hour Aberdeen–Glasgow Buchanan Street expresses. It was withdrawn on 1 May 1966 and passed into preservation. **Date: 24 October 1964.**

↑ The 'Solway Ranger' railtour, organised by the West Riding branch of the RCTS, was a memorable day out. This provided 364 miles with steam, including rebuilt 'Merchant Navy' No 35012 *United States Line* over Shap and Ais Gill, two Ivatt 2MT 2-6-0s, and the Scottish preserved locomotives No 123, the 'Caley Single', and No 49 *Gordon Highlander*. The train is shown at Silloth, which was due to lose its services in less than three months.

The Great North of Scotland Railway had 21 4-4-0s built, of Classes F and V, which were very similar, 18 of which entered BR service. No 49 (BR No 62277) was new in 1920 and lasted until June 1958, when it was sent to Inverurie Works for attention, emerging in the GNSR green livery (which it had never carried), and for a short time resumed duties on the Speyside line. It was then moved to Dawsholm shed (65D) at Glasgow, from where it operated specials. The 'Caley Single' was built by Neilson & Co in 1886 and its claim to fame was that it took part in the famous 'Races to the North' in 1888 and 1895. It was classified as 1P and numbered 14010 by the LMS and withdrawn in 1935. It then spent about 20 years in St Rollox Works, which included the war years, before being returned to traffic to work specials in 1957. It is now in the new Riverside Museum in Glasgow.
Date: 23 May 1964.

⬆ The Highland Railway 'Jones Goods' No 103, was the fourth Scottish locomotive to be returned to working order in the late 1950s. It was built by Sharp Stewart in 1894 and remained in service on the Highland lines until October 1934. It then vanished from public view, inside the paint shop at St Rollox Works, until being returned to working order in 1958. It is shown on Holbeck shed (55A) at Leeds and was the most unusual locomotive I ever saw on the shed.

This pioneer 4-6-0 was returning from Bedford, where it had been taking part in the filming of *Those Magnificent Men in their Flying Machines*, being disguised as a French locomotive and numbered 23. It was on its way back to Glasgow and the shed staff kindly ran it up and down the yard for me to get photographs. I was the only enthusiast present (how times have changed). It is now in the Riverside Museum, Glasgow. **Date: 25 May 1964.**

↑ The 'Gainsborough Model Railway Society' special arrived at Aberystwyth on this day with nine coaches, for a visit to the 11¾ mile 1ft 11½in gauge Vale of Rheidol Railway, which needed two trains for all the passengers. The specials are seen ready to leave the station at Aberystwyth with No 8 *Llywelyn* and No 9 *Prince of Wales*. An Act of Parliament was passed for the construction of the line in 1897 in two stages; the first to Devil's Bridge, followed by the harbour branch. Traffic peaked in 1912 and a decline set in with the harbour branch closing in 1939. The railway became BR's last steam operation until it was privatised in 1989, since when it has become a major tourist attraction in Wales. The locomotive fleet of Nos 7, 8 and 9 were built at Swindon Works, although No 9 was claimed to be a rebuild, but it has been proved that this was for internal administration reasons and was in fact a new locomotive. All three are still currently working the services. **Date: 30 May 1964.**

↗ A familiar sight at Bournemouth was, for at least 20 years, the 'unrebuilt' 'West Country' and 'Battle of Britain' classes, leaving on up Waterloo expresses, which very often produced a fair amount of slipping on the tight curve. Here, we have the unique member of the classes No 34064 *Fighter Command* (the 1,000th locomotive to be built at Brighton Works), which was fitted with a Giesl ejector during its last general overhaul at Eastleigh Works in April 1962.

Reports seem to vary on how much the modification improved the performance, some suggesting it was then equal to a 'Merchant Navy' but, what it did achieve, was a big reduction in coal consumption due to virtually eliminating the throwing of live embers from the chimney or lifting the fire. Whatever the results, it was the only one to be treated and retained the modification until withdrawn on 22 May 1966, with a claimed mileage of 759,666 miles in 19 years of service. **Date: 9 September 1964.**

→ There were 25 of these fine mixed-traffic Class S15 4-6-0s built in two batches between 1927 and 1936. They were similar to the famous 'King Arthur' class in looks which, like both classes, was rather old fashioned with the Urie-designed tender, and quite modern with the six- and eight-wheeled bogie design. They were excellent locomotives, which gave fine service on both freight and passenger duties and they outlived the 'King Arthurs'. No 30838 is leaving Southampton with an afternoon stopping train for Bournemouth and is attached to a flat-sided bogie tender. No 30838 continued in service until 19 September 1965. **Date: 11 September 1964.**

⬆ A well-cleaned Eastleigh rebuilt 'West Country', No 34104 *Bere Alston*, is heading a down express round the triangle from Gas Works Junction to Bournemouth West Junction, just outside Bournemouth West station. No 34104 was the last of the class to be built at Eastleigh Works, in April 1950, and the last to be rebuilt, in May 1961. Records show it only travelled 252,876 miles as a rebuilt engine, before being withdrawn from Eastleigh (71A) shed in June 1967.
Date: 9 September 1964.

⬆ After covering the 79 miles non-stop with the heavy down 'Bournemouth Belle', the fireman is just replacing the water column bag after the immaculate rebuilt 'Merchant Navy', No 35022 *Holland-America Line* has taken water at Southampton Central. No 35022 was a Western Division locomotive of the Southern Region for its entire career, covering a total of 903,542 miles from new in October 1948. It was rebuilt in June 1956 and was withdrawn in May 1966 and ended up in Woodham's scrapyard at Barry, where it remained for 20 years before being rescued, although it has not as yet been restored to working order. The 'Bournemouth Belle' Pullman train first ran on 5 July 1931, with the last titled train running on 9 July 1967, although it was withdrawn during the war years. **Date: 12 September 1964.**

⬆ The fine clock tower at Southampton Central is showing 11.45am, above the 'unrebuilt' 'West Country' No 34105 *Swanage*, which is ready to leave with a down cross-country express after taking water. No 34105 entered service in March 1950 and was allocated to Bournemouth shed (71B), where it remained until being reallocated to Eastleigh, during the weekend this picture was taken. Withdrawal came one month later on 4 October 1964. It passed into preservation at the Mid-Hants Railway, where it was restored to working order. **Date: 12 September 1964.**

This scene, of a Class O2 smokebox being cleaned of ash at Ventnor, Isle of Wight, after the journey from Ryde, has been captured many times before. No 35 *Freshwater* is seen alongside the water column receiving attention. Details of the O2 0-4-4Ts and their long association with IoW lines are given on page 76. No 35 lasted in service until 1 October 1966. **Date: 5 September 1964.**

The nameplate attached to Isle of Wight Class O2 No 35. **Date: 5 September 1964.**

⬆ On the ex-L&YR route from Halifax to Bradford Exchange (now Interchange), between the closed stations of Lightcliffe (14 June 1965) and Wyke (21 September 1953), is the seldom-photographed Hall Bottom Viaduct. Ex-Leeds Holbeck (1950–62) 'Jubilee' No 45565 *Victoria*, now allocated to Low Moor shed (56F), is seen crossing with an evening freight from Halifax, which contained wagons destined for London.

No 45565, built by the North British Loco Co in 1934, was allocated to a wide variety of sheds before arriving at Leeds Holbeck. It was withdrawn in January 1967, apparently in good condition and it was said that it was considered for preservation, but due to it needing a new ashpan, it was rejected as this would have cost too much to replace. **Date: 2 July 1964.**

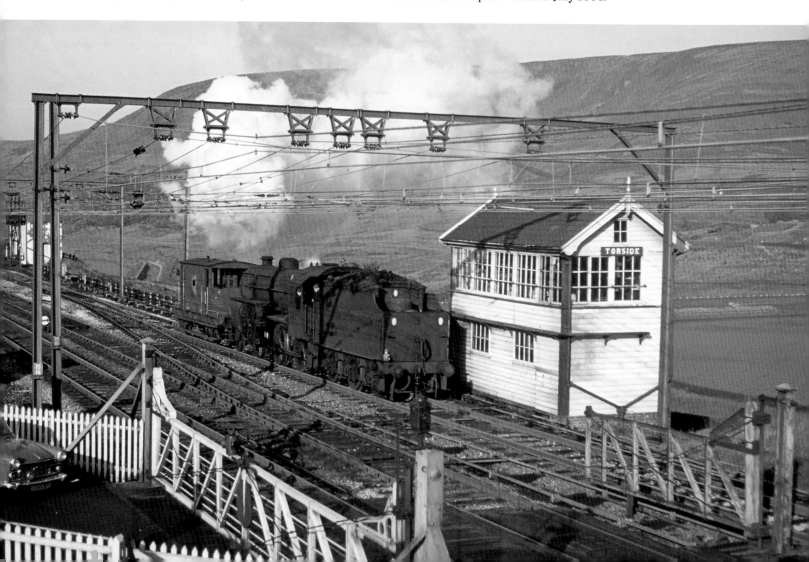

⬆ The line, from Shipley to Laisterdyke via Idle, was used for getting freight across Bradford and was an ex-Great Northern route with the terminus at Shipley & Windhill, which closed in 1931. This fine Great Northern somersault signal was at Shipley. The line closed in two sections: Laisterdyke to Quarry Gap on 28 October 1966, and Shipley to Idle on 5 October 1968. 'Jubilee' No 45694 *Bellerophon*, which had been on the Holbeck allocation for 20 years except for one month, moved to Low Moor in 1962 and at weekends was used on trains to Blackpool and other seaside locations. During the week it could be seen on humble freight duties. Here, it is leaving Shipley, passing the somersault signal with an evening freight. No 45694 was withdrawn from Wakefield shed (56A) in 1967. **Date: 1 September 1964.**

⬅ The sight of a steam locomotive on the electrified Woodhead route at Torside was rare at this time. I was on my way to a funeral in Worcester and was stopped at the level crossing gates at Torside, expecting a Class 76 electric loco on a coal train when I noticed steam approaching. I grabbed the camera from the car boot (never travel without a camera – you never know what you may see) and obtained this picture. What this 'Crab' 2-6-0, No 42715, was doing, I never found out, but it certainly would not have travelled through the new Woodhead Tunnel. No 42715 was allocated to Gorton shed in Manchester at the time and was withdrawn on 30 January 1966. **Date: 23 October 1964.**

⬆ After its epic performance over Grayrigg and Shap banks in the morning, with the famous Nine Elms driver Bert Hooker at the regulator, 'Merchant Navy' No 35012 *United States Line* made its way to Carlisle Kingmoor shed for servicing, before giving another memorable performance over Ais Gill Summit. The immaculate locomotive is seen on the shed and I believe this is the furthest north a 'Merchant Navy' Pacific has ever been.

It entered service on 13 January 1945 numbered 21C12 and was allocated to Nine Elms and Bournemouth sheds for its entire career, except for around 2½ years at Weymouth, from September 1964. It was rebuilt in February 1957 having only covered 564,821 miles since new, and went on to reach a total of 1,134,836 miles before being withdrawn in April 1967. **Date: 13 June 1964.**

↗ Details of the unique Giesl ejector fitted to 'Battle of Britain' No 34064 *Fighter Command* have been given on page 115. Here it is seen on Eastleigh shed (71A) between duties, so fitted. **Date: 12 September 1964.**

➡ This is a view of the up 'Bournemouth Belle', is ready to leave Bournemouth West station with rebuilt 'Merchant Navy' No 35017 *Belgian Marine*. It was new in April 1945, numbered 21C17, and was allocated to Nine Elms shed (70A) until 1964. It then moved to Weymouth for the rest of its career, which ended in July after it had run 1,017,754 miles. Before it was rebuilt in March 1957, it was one of the locomotives which took part in the Locomotive Exchanges in 1948, when it was attached to a Stanier tender to provide a water scoop. The other two Ivatt 2-6-2Ts in the picture are Nos 41270 and 41214. The latter is on a Somerset & Dorset service to Templecombe. **Date: 15 September 1964.**

By the beginning of 1964 there were only three of the famous Somerset & Dorset 2-8-0s left in service. The Home Counties Railway Society organised a farewell tour for the class using No 53807 and an original S&DJR Fowler 0-6-0 4F, No 44558. No 53807 was the last of the 7Fs to be withdrawn on 24 August 1964. The tour started from Bournemouth and headed for Highbridge then returned to Evercreech Junction, before tackling the 1-in-50 gradients to Masbury Summit. In what was otherwise a miserable day, the sun came out for a few minutes at Evercreech Junction to the delight of the passengers. **Date: 7 June 1964.**

↑ One of the auto-fitted ex-Great Western 6400 class 0-6-0 pannier tanks, No 6430, is working the shuttle service between Yeovil Town (which closed to passengers on 2 October 1966) and Yeovil Junction. No 6430 was allocated to Yeovil Town shed (83E) in November 1963 and withdrawn in October 1964, with the shed closing in 1965. **Date: 17 September 1964.**

After ten years (1951 to 1961) working the expresses out of Liverpool Street, 'Britannia' 4-6-2 No 70006 *Robert Burns* moved to March shed (31B) for two years before heading north to Carlisle Kingmoor shed (12A). The majority of the class worked out their time there for a few years, on a variety of duties before being withdrawn, in the case of No 70006, on 20 May 1967. Only seven weeks after being transferred to Carlisle, and looking quite clean for a Kingmoor 'Britannia', it makes an impressive sight as it passes the signalbox at Dent station (Britain's highest station at 1,145ft) with a down freight. **Date: 18 January 1964.**

After suffering a failure by a 'Britannia' Pacific earlier in the day, which was replaced by a Stanier Class 5 (see page 131), the Warwickshire Railway Society special prepares to leave the yard alongside Kingmoor shed and head south over the Settle & Carlisle route behind rebuilt 'Royal Scot' No 46160 *Queen Victoria's Rifleman*. It was built in 1930, rebuilt with a taper boiler in February 1945, and withdrawn on 1 May 1965 with a recorded mileage of 1,940,125 up to the end of 1960. **Date: 28 November 1964.**

↑ The 733 WD class 2-8-0s were rare on passenger workings, no doubt much to the relief of the crews, but they occasionally turned up on empty stock movements, mainly in the summer months. Here, we see such an occasion with No 90641 heading north at Morecambe South Junction on the West Coast Main Line, taking the line to Morecambe. It was a very lengthy train, which I believe was 16 coaches. After the war, No 90641 was allocated to the Southern Region, but moved to the London Midland in July 1951 at Newton Heath in Manchester (26A). By the date of the photograph it was at Aintree shed (8L), from where it was withdrawn on 17 July 1965. **Date: 29 August 1964.**

→ One of the 221 Fowler 3F 0-6-0Ts, or 'Jinties' as they were known, is going about its unglamorous shunting duties in Carnforth yard. No 47662 was allocated to Carnforth in April 1964, but moved on after 13 months, eventually being withdrawn on 1 January 1966. **Date: 26 August 1964.**

↑ By 1964, virtually all the 'Princess Coronation' duties had been taken over by the diesel-electrics, so the class was frequently seen on parcels trains and even freights. No 46225 *Duchess of Gloucester* is at Carnforth at the Barrow-in-Furness platform on 3L14, the 13.40 Crewe–Carlisle parcels train which, as it was heading north, had to reverse out of the station.

In spite of its clean appearance, No 46225 only had another three weeks left in service and was probably one of the several members of the class that were withdrawn when in good mechanical order. Withdrawal came on 12 September 1964 with the locomotive being credited with 1,609,518 miles during its 26-year career. **Date: 26 August 1964.**

↘ One of the most interesting trains that ran in West Yorkshire was the Heaton–Red Bank empty newspaper van train, which comprised all the vans carrying the newspapers to the North East from Manchester the previous night. It was usually loaded to around 23 vans and needed double heading over the Pennines. What made it so interesting was the variety of motive power and the different combinations used. West of Leeds I saw at least 12 different classes in all combinations. On the eastern side of Leeds, Eastern Region Pacifics were frequently used. On one occasion, I saw a Llandudno Junction Class 5 piloting a Gateshead A4. It was not a very good time keeper, but generally passed through Sowerby Bridge, where it is shown, between 4.30pm and 5pm. The Stanier Moguls were not all that common in the area, but occasionally turned up on this working, as seen here with Class 5 No 45229 of Aintree shed (8L) piloting Stanier 2-6-0 No 42955 of Nuneaton (5E). No 45229 lasted until 17 July 1965, and 42955 until 23 March 1966. **Date: 24 July 1964.**

← The Bradford portion of a Leeds–King's Cross express is climbing the 1-in-50 gradient to Hall Lane, just outside Bradford Exchange, headed by Fairburn tank No 42142. Fowler 2-6-4T No 42410 waits to reverse some empty stock down into the station. In total, 125 of the very successful Fowler tanks were built between 1927 and 1934, with No 42410 becoming the last in service, being withdrawn on 13 August 1966. It had been allocated to Huddersfield's Hillhouse shed since 1950 at least. **Date: 21 August 1964.**

⬆ As explained on page 126, the 1X82 Warwickshire Railway Society special to Carlisle to visit Kingmoor shed suffered a failure at Carnforth with 'Britannia' No 70052. This resulted in this rather dirty Class 5, No 45018, taking over, but it was probably in better condition than it looked, as it was making very good progress up Shap unaided with a ten-coach load.

Over the years, No 45018 was allocated to Carlisle Kingmoor several times and was on that allocation at the time this picture was taken. The 4-6-0 was eventually withdrawn from the shed on 31 December 1966. **Date: 28 November 1964.**

◤ During the construction of the last batch of the 125 Fowler 2-6-4Ts in 1934, Stanier was in charge and he incorporated a few modifications, such as side-window cabs, improved bogies, and flat side rods. One of the duties that will always be associated with this batch of the class was the banking of trains up Shap, with the locomotives being allocated to Tebay shed. The class was gradually replaced on this work in the early 1960s by Fairburn 2-6-4Ts as the Fowler examples were withdrawn. No 42414 is working hard, banking a freight near Scout Green, about halfway up the hill. No 42414 arrived at Tebay in December 1961, after working in the West Riding of Yorkshire for many years and was withdrawn on 3 October 1964, a week after this picture was taken. **Date: 26 September 1964.**

◄ On a glorious winter's day near Scout Green on Shap, Fairburn 2-6-4T No 42210 is shown banking a freight up the hill. This was one of the class which had arrived at Tebay shed to replace the Fowler 2-6-4Ts, its reallocation being made in June 1964. It continued as a Shap banker until withdrawn on 22 April 1967, with steam officially ending in December 1967 over Shap, when Tebay shed closed. **Date: 28 November 1964.**

1965

The main event of the year was probably the elimination of steam from the Western Region. The last booked steam working out of Paddington was on 11 June to Banbury, although an official farewell to steam special ran on 27 November, with both trains being hauled by No 7029 *Clun Castle*. This, of course, marked the end for the 'Halls', 'Castles', 'Granges' and 'Manors', as well as some other ex-GWR classes. Vast numbers of steam locomotives were being withdrawn from all the regions, including the last rebuilt 'Royal Scot' and 'Patriot'. The major scrap yards at Barry, Bridgend, Kettering, Long Marston, Newport Gwent, Hull, Troon, Beighton, Great Bridge, Killamarsh, Motherwell and Airdrie were full. It was not only the locomotives that were vanishing, but a lot of railway infrastructure, with the famous Crumlin Viaduct in South Wales being dismantled.

In my own area of the north of England, things had changed dramatically as far as steam activity was concerned. The services from Leeds to King's Cross were in the hands of the 'Deltics' and Brush Type 4s. The Trans-Pennine services, from Leeds to Manchester via Huddersfield or Halifax, were all diesel, either DMUs or locomotives. In the North East, the BR 9F 2-10-0s finished on the Consett iron ore trains.

There was one high-profile event for steam, which was Sir Winston Churchill's funeral train being hauled by 'Battle of Britain' No 34051 *Winston Churchill*, on 30 January from Waterloo to Handborough.

The Beeching closures continued with around 43 lines and services going. The following were the main closures:

Lostwithiel–Fowey 4 January
Chippenham–Calne 20 April
Barnstaple–Torrington and Halwill Junction 4 October
Axminster–Lyme Regis 29 November
Yeovil Town–Yeovil Pen Mill 29 November
West Drayton–Staines West 29 March
Dunstable–Hatfield 26 April
Guildford–Christ's Hospital 14 June
Eridge–Hailsham 14 June
Lincoln–Grantham 1 November
Uttoxeter–Leek 4 January
Water Orton–Wolverhampton 18 January
Burton-on-Trent–Wolverhampton 18 January
Walsall–Rugeley (Trent Valley) via Cannock 18 January
Whitchurch–Welshpool 18 January
Llanmynech–Llanfyllin 18 January
Ruabon–Barmouth and Bala–Bala Junction 18 January
Bishop Auckland–Crook 8 March
Scarborough–Whitby 8 March
Grosmont–Malton 8 March
Skipton–Ilkley 22 March
Low Moor–Mirfield (via Cleckheaton) 14 June

Ulverston–Lakeside 5 September
Blackrod/Lostock Junction–Horwich 27 September
Earby–Barnoldswick 27 September
Rose Grove–Todmorden 1 November
York–Beverley via Market Weighton 29 November
Driffield–Selby via Market Weighton 29 November
Maud Junction–Peterhead 3 May
Fraserburgh–St Combs 3 May
Ballinluig–Aberfeldy 3 May
Castle Douglas–Kirkcudbright 3 May
Dumfries–Challoch Junction via Castle Douglas 14 June
St Andrews–Leven 6 September
Dunblane–Crianlarich 27 September
Killin–Killin Junction 27 September
Dyce–Fraserburgh 4 October
Haughead Junction (Hamilton)–Coalburn 4 October
(Hamilton–Larkhall since reopened)
Strathaven–Stonehouse 4 October
Crosshouse–Irvine 11 October
Aviemore–Forres 18 October
Boat of Garten–Craigellachie 18 October
Kilmacolm–Princess Pier 30 November

As one can see, Scotland suffered badly. There were some important developments too, such as the opening of Tinsley Yard with the 700hp twin diesel shunters (later Class 13). A new diesel depot opened at Old Oak Common, and the Class AM 10 EMUs started working into Euston on commuter services, from 25 October.

The areas of steam activity were getting smaller, but there was still much worse to come.

⬆ Here is an everyday scene on a shed, of a locomotive having the water tanks topped up, before leaving to work its diagram. Ivatt 2-6-2T No 41283 of Templecombe shed (83G) looks as if it has had a recent visit to Eastleigh Works for an overhaul. It was new to Wakefield shed (25A later 56A) in October 1950 and then moved around the London Midland Region, before being reallocated to Brighton in June 1961.

After transfer to other Southern sheds, it was moved to Templecombe in April 1965 on the Western Region, from where it was withdrawn on 20 February 1966. **Date: 8 September 1965.**

↑ Rebuilt 'Royal Scot' No 46115 *Scots Guardsman*'s main claim to fame, before preservation, was that it was the first example of the rebuilds to be fitted with smoke deflectors in 1947. It is seen at Hellifield station after taking water and is ready to depart on the RCTS 'Rebuilt Scot Commemorative Rail Tour', which ran from Crewe to Carlisle via the Settle & Carlisle, returning via Shap. The locomotive booked for the tour was No 46160 *Queen Victoria's Rifleman*, but it had failed on Leeds Holbeck shed and No 46115 was substituted at the last minute. It had been well cleaned by Crewe North shed and fitted with wooden nameplates.

While at Hellifield, the passengers were allowed to visit the shed, which was under the control of the Museum of Transport and housed several locomotives being stored for the National Collection. The yellow stripe on the cabside of No 46115 indicated that the locomotive was banned from working south of Crewe under the wires. This was the last of the rebuilt 'Royal Scots' to be withdrawn, on 1 January 1966, when it passed into preservation.

Apart from working a couple of specials when it was based at Dinting, enthusiasts had to wait 43 years before it was seen back on the main line on a regular basis, but the wait was well worth it. **Date: 13 February 1965.**

↖ Hellifield shed closed in 1963 so the snow plough duties, especially for keeping the Settle & Carlisle clear, were transferred to Skipton. The large snow plough is fitted to Fowler 0-6-0 4F No 44276, which had been allocated to Hellifield shed since at least 1950 and then transferred to Skipton when the former closed. No 44276 stayed at Skipton until withdrawn on 24 April 1965. **Date: 2 March 1965.**

← Skipton shed's code changed four times between 1950 and 1963, namely: 23A, 20F, 24G and finally 10G when it closed in 1967. It had two of the BR Standard 2-6-2T 2MT class 84000 series on its allocation. No 84015 arrived in July 1958 and No 84028 in September 1961. One of the duties for which they were diagrammed was the Barnoldswick branch, which lost its passenger services on 27 September 1965. After that the 84000s were retained for the freight turn, but these ceased on 1 August 1966. The tanks then left for Eastleigh (71A) to be prepared for replacing the Class O2 0-4-4Ts on the Isle of Wight, but they never reached there, and on paper, at least, they were transferred back to Skipton and withdrawn. No 84028 is shown on the shed's turntable. **Date: 2 March 1965.**

The Stephenson Locomotive Society organised the 'Whitby Moors Rail Tour', which travelled over the Pennines via the Calder Valley route through Halifax, eventually arriving at Gascoigne Wood. 'Jubilee' class 4-6-0 No 45698 *Mars* was then exchanged for the preserved K4 class 2-6-0 No 3442 *The Great Marquess*, piloting K1 No 62005 (also now preserved), which headed off to Market Weighton. En route to Scarborough, the Filey Holiday Camp line was visited. The main attraction of the tour was to traverse the scenic Scarborough–Whitby line, which was to close completely from that day. After reversal at Whitby Cliff station, which had closed in 1961, the special reversed down the bank to Whitby Town. The train then returned via the North Yorkshire Moors line. The special is shown at Staintondale. **Date: 6 March 1965.**

The 'Whitby Moors Rail Tour' is crossing Larpool Viaduct, also known as Esk Valley Viaduct, which was built between October 1882 and 24 October 1884, with the line opening in July 1885. It is now a Grade 2 listed structure and carries a cycle path. It has 13 arches on 12 piers, is 915ft long and 120ft high above the river. It is estimated that 5,000,000 bricks were used, and that it weighs 26,000 tons. **Date: 6 March 1965.**

→ The elegant preserved Great North of Scotland Railway Class D40 (LNER classification) No 49 *Gordon Highlander*, worked a special around Lanarkshire and then travelled across to the Edinburgh area, where it visited the branch which used to go to Glencorse, but only went as far as Roslin. The line went to a colliery starting at Millerhill and was steeply graded. This proved too much for the locomotive, which stalled opposite where I was standing near Loanhead but after a 'blow up', it continued to Roslin. Passenger services had been withdrawn from the line in 1933.
Date: 16 October 1965.

↓ In the early days of the preservation of No 4472 *Flying Scotsman*, arrived at Cheadle Heath on a special run by the Locomotive Club of Great Britain, the 'High Peak Rail Tour', where it came off and was replaced by 'Jubilee' No 45705 *Seahorse*, which continued the journey to Buxton.
Date: 18 September 1965.

We now live in times when steam locomotives running on the preserved and main lines all look as if they have come out of a works paint shop the previous day. Back in the 1960s, there were many examples when they appeared in terrible external condition and one of the worst I saw was green-liveried 'Britannia' No 70028 *Royal Star*, allocated to Crewe North shed (5A). It is shown on Leeds Holbeck (55A). No 70028 had been one of the locomotives loaned to Exmouth Junction shed (72A) by Cardiff Canton (86C), to help out the Southern Region, when the 'Merchant Navy' class had to be withdrawn, after No 35020 *Bibby Line* fractured a crank axle at 80mph. No 70028 was withdrawn from Carlisle Kingmoor shed (12A) on 16 September 1967. **Date: 25 March 1965.**

What used to be an everyday scene at the end of main line station platforms were groups of schoolboys enjoying themselves watching the trains and writing down the engine numbers, probably with the help of an Ian Allan ABC pocket book. Few young boys seem to do it these days, although there are still groups at certain locations, where the average age appears to have increased dramatically, many sitting on chairs, with flasks, talking into tape recorders. I must confess to keeping a record of which locomotives and units I have in my photographic collection. This scene was taken at the north end of Lancaster Castle station of 'Britannia' No 70012 *John of Gaunt* at the head of the 10.30 Euston–Carlisle. It is interesting to see that it is running in an unlined green livery. No 70012 was eventually withdrawn on 30 December 1967. **Date: 9 October 1965.**

⬆ Class A4 No 60009 *Union of South Africa* was new to Haymarket shed (64B) in June 1937, and it remained on the allocation for 25 years, becoming the shed's most famous A4. In May 1962, it was transferred to Aberdeen Ferryhill (61B), where it worked the three-hour Glasgow–Aberdeen expresses, until it was withdrawn on 1 June 1966 and bought for preservation by Mr John Cameron. It was kept in its purpose-built shed at the Lochty Private Railway. It moved from Lochty and eventually started running main line specials and visiting preserved railways, which it has continued to do ever since. In this picture, it is passing Perth shed (63A) with a morning up express from Aberdeen to Glasgow Buchanan Street.
Date: 13 August 1965.

⬆ This is a view taken in the yard at Perth shed, looking north and showing Class A4 No 60019 *Bittern* and ex-North British Railway Class J37 No 64621. In the distance, 'Britannia' No 70038 and Class 5 4-6-0 No 45473 are ready to go off the shed. Perth (63A) was a fine shed and in 1950 had an allocation of 138 locomotives, 75 of which were Stanier Class 5s. By 1965, the total had dropped to 29, owing to the invasion of various Type 2 diesels. No 60019 was never one of the high-profile members of the class, spending 26 years at the Newcastle sheds of Gateshead and Heaton.

Bittern then moved to Aberdeen Ferryhill, initially spending one month at St Margaret's shed (64A) and settling down to working the three-hour Glasgow Buchanan Street–Aberdeen expresses, until withdrawn on 5 September 1966. It was bought by G.S. Drury and passed into preservation. After many years in store, it has finally started working main line specials, recently running as No 4492 *Dominion of New Zealand*. Class J37 No 64621's less glamorous career had already ended three months previously, on 1 May 1965. **Date: 13 August 1965.**

After the 'Pines Express' was diverted away from the Somerset & Dorset route in September 1962, it travelled via Southampton and Oxford. It was normally worked by a Bournemouth 'West Country' or 'Battle of Britain', but on this occasion, 'Merchant Navy' No 35003 *Royal Mail* was in charge. It is seen climbing the 1-in-176 bank across Brockenhurst Common, with a complete set of maroon coaches. The last time the 'Pines' ran as a titled train was on 4 March 1967. The Lymington branch can just be seen in the far distance.

Originally numbered 21C3 when new in September 1941, *Royal Mail* was rebuilt during a general overhaul in September 1959. It was withdrawn from Nine Elms shed (70A) in July 1967, with records showing it had travelled 1,131,793 miles during its 26-year career. **Date: 9 September 1965.**

The Q1 class 'Austerity' 0-6-0 was designed by O.V.S. Bulleid in 1942. There were 40 built at Brighton and Ashford Works during the year and numbered C1 to C40. They were designed for wartime conditions, when the Southern Railway was involved in carrying far more freight than in peacetime. It was to be expected that the design would be unconventional and weight reduction was a major consideration. The boiler was designed for the maximum size possible within the loading gauge and to give the driver a good enough view. The result was a powerful lightweight 0-6-0, with a tractive effort of 30,000lb at 85 per cent boiler pressure, which was 230lb. They were good locomotives, powerful and fast. Speeds of 75mph were claimed, although the sight of the side rods, which were visible from the cab spinning round at such a speed, alarmed some crews.

The LCGB 'Vectis Rail Tour', which came from London to Chichester, travelled on the Lavant branch using Nos 33020 and 33027 in top-and-tail mode. No 33027 is pulling the stock out of Chichester station in order to attach No 33020 at the other end. The tour continued to Portsmouth, where the passengers crossed to the Isle of Wight for a trip from Ryde to Ventnor. Both locomotives were withdrawn on 14 December 1965. **Date: 3 October 1965.**

⬆ Another excellent rail tour was organised by the Stephenson Locomotive Society, starting at Birmingham Snow Hill and running to Salisbury, Exeter and Westbury, and return. The most famous of the 'unrebuilt' 'Battle of Britain' class, No 34051 *Winston Churchill*, was the selected locomotive to haul the tour to Salisbury, which was its home shed. A stop was made at Leamington for water and photographs, where this shot was taken of it, alongside the fine signals at the south end of the station. 'Merchant Navy' No 35017 *Belgian Marine* took over at Salisbury for a fast run to Exeter Central and on to Westbury, where GWR 4-6-0 No 7029 *Clun Castle* was waiting for the return to Birmingham.

No 34051 only had four months left in service at the time of this tour, being withdrawn on 19 September 1965 with a recorded final mileage of 807,496. It then passed into the NRM collection, but has never returned to service, as there are so many other examples now in working order. **Date: 23 May 1965.**

As mentioned in the previous pages, 'Battle of Britain' No 34051 *Winston Churchill* was withdrawn on 19 September 1965, and by 10 December it arrived at Leeds Holbeck shed en route to Hellifield shed for safe storage. BR Class 5MT 4-6-0 No 73112 is coupled in front of No 34051 and should have been detached at a scrapyard in Sheffield on the journey north, but finished up on Holbeck shed by mistake. **Date: 10 December 1965.**

The Warwickshire Railway Society organised a tour over the Settle & Carlisle on 11 December 1965, and Holbeck 'Jubilee' No 45697 *Achilles* was diagrammed to take it over from Leeds to Carlisle. No 45697 was no stranger to the S&C, as it was allocated to Carlisle Kingmoor shed for ten years, between 1952 and 1962, before reaching Holbeck in March 1964, where it stayed until withdrawn in September 1967. The special is approaching Belle Busk, in low winter sunshine, where there had been a station until passenger and goods services were withdrawn on 4 May 1959, but at this date the signalbox was still open. **Date: 11 December 1965.**

1966

This was another very busy year photographically, as classes became extinct but, more importantly, there were one or two high-profile line closures. For me, the end of the Somerset & Dorset was a big blow, as I was very late in getting to know the line and realising what I had been missing over the years. However, as the selection of pictures for 1966 show, I did my best to cover many of the specials that ran between January and March. The other major withdrawal was the end of through services on the old Great Central main line, just leaving semi-fast trains running between Rugby and Nottingham. This meant the end of railway centres, such as Woodford Halse, where the community had developed around the railway over the years. Steam also finished on the Isle of Wight.

There were large areas of the country where steam had been eliminated, but with the Waterloo–Bournemouth–Weymouth services almost entirely steam worked, there was still somewhere for enthusiasts to go and travel behind main line steam. As time progressed towards their end in July, the performances seemed to get better and better. In the rest of the country, most of the passenger steam workings were concentrated in the North West and West Yorkshire.

The rate of withdrawals got faster and faster, with the main scrap merchants stockpiling locomotives for scrap. There were about 150 locomotives at Woodham's in Barry, and fortunately, most of those there finished up in preservation.

Services from two Glasgow main stations, namely St Enoch and Buchanan Street, ended. At the other end of the country, Southampton Terminus also closed. Some famous sheds closed to steam including Carlisle Upperby, Doncaster, Leicester Midland and Llandudno Junction, to highlight a few. For LNER enthusiasts it was a disastrous year, as the A1, A2, A3 and A4 class Pacifics all became extinct on BR.

There were another couple of notable events: first the opening on 18 April of full electric services between London Euston, Manchester and Liverpool, and another was the death of Sir William Stanier at the age of 89.

The list of closures and withdrawal of services was not as great numerically as some years but, as already mentioned, included some important lines and stations:

Evercreech Junction–Highbridge 7 March
Bath Green Park–Bournemouth 7 March
Mangotsfield–Bath Green Park 7 March
Seaton Junction–Seaton 7 March
Holt Junction–Patney via Devizes 18 April
Yeovil Town–Yeovil Junction 3 October
Taunton–Barnstaple 3 October
Halwill Junction–Bude 3 October
Halwill Junction–Wadebridge 3 October
Totton–Fawley 14 February
Smallbrook Junction–Cowes 21 February
Christ's Hospital–Shoreham 7 March
Shanklin–Ventnor 18 April
Saxmundham–Aldeburgh 12 April
Rugby–Peterborough 6 June

Seaton–Stamford 6 June
Nottingham–Kettering 6 June
Aylesbury–Rugby 5 September
Banbury–Woodford Halse 5 September
Nottingham Victoria–Sheffield Victoria 5 September
Gobowen–Oswestry 7 November
Wennington–Lancaster Green Ayre–Morecambe
  3 January
Keswick–Workington 18 April
Rawtenstall–Bacup 5 December
Bury–Stubbins Junction–Accrington 5 December
Aberdeen–Ballater 28 February
Connel Ferry–Ballachulish 28 March
Dalry–Kilmarnock 18 April
Lochwinnoch Loop 27 June

Such a list makes depressing reading. I decided to make my first railway-only trip abroad, to Germany for five days, which covered about 2,500 miles and I saw a lot of impressive sights. However, it made me realise how elegant most of our British locomotives were compared with the Continental types, which had everything attached to the outside and, in some cases, had chimneys that looked like dustbins, but that is another matter entirely.

⬆ BR Class 4MT 4-6-0 No 75072 was new in September 1955 and was allocated to Exmouth Junction (72A) for nine months, before moving to the Somerset & Dorset line, where it spent the rest of its career. Two reliable records show it as being withdrawn on 31 December 1965. It certainly looks fit for withdrawal but here it is seen leaving Evercreech Junction on 1 January 1966 on a stopping train for Bath. It was probably being moved from Templecombe to Bath shed for storage, where it had been officially allocated, so it is likely that this was its very last working. **Date: 1 January 1966.**

⬆ After 112 years, Glastonbury and Street station has only another two months to go before closure, on 7 March 1966. Ivatt 2-6-2T No 41290 is ready to leave with a local service to Templecombe via Evercreech Junction. New in November 1951, No 41290 was initially allocated to Crewe North shed but was eventually sent to Templecombe (83G), in November 1964, where it stayed until withdrawn. **Date: 1 January 1966.**

⬆ On the last day of regular services on the S&D line, the Locomotive Club of Great Britain ran a special over the line from Templecombe to Bath and back. The special arrived at Templecombe behind 'Merchant Navy' No 35028 *Clan Line* (now preserved), where two Ivatt 2-6-2Ts, Nos 41307 and 41249, took over for a trip to Highbridge and back to Evercreech Junction. Here, an immaculate 'West Country', No 34006 *Bude* and 'Battle of Britain' No 34057 *Biggin Hill*, also very well turned out, were waiting to take the train to Bath. They are seen in the centre road at Evercreech Junction awaiting the arrival of the special.

No 34006 was one of the locomotives which took part in the locomotive exchanges in 1948, when it was fitted with extra-long smoke deflectors, as seen in this picture, compared to No 34057. It retained them until it was withdrawn on 19 March 1967, when it became one of the very few members of the class to exceed one million miles in service. In fact, at 1,099,338 miles, it was the highest for the class. Both locomotives were allocated to Salisbury at the time of the tour, with No 34057 being withdrawn on 7 May 1967 with a total of 939,597 miles recorded. **Date: 5 March 1966.**

⬆ The Stanier 8F 2-8-0s were seen on the old S&DJR after August 1964, with the arrival of No 48309, and two more coming the following year. No 48309 worked an LCGB special on 4 April 1965, but they were not used on passenger work on a regular basis. Bath shed must have been desperately short of usable locomotives on the last day of services to turn out 8F No 48760 for the morning stopping service from Bath to Templecombe. As I followed it south it appeared to perform well and I obtained this picture of it emerging from the morning mist as it entered Midsomer Norton station. Along with several other Stanier 8Fs, they were transferred to the Western Region, due to regional boundary changes, in 1950. No 48760 only arrived on the Bath allocation in July 1965 and is recorded as being withdrawn on 29 January 1966, but had obviously been reinstated. **Date: 5 March 1966.**

↑ 'Britannia' No 70052 *Firth of Tay* is seen 104ft off the ground, over one of the 24, 45ft span arches of Ribblehead Viaduct, heading the 12 noon all-stations Hellifield–Carlisle stopping train. The viaduct is the longest, at 440 yards, on the Settle & Carlisle railway and construction was started in 1870, and completed in 1874.

Firth of Tay had an unfortunate connection with the Settle & Carlisle line, as it was the locomotive which caused the accident at Langcliffe, just north of Settle, when at 1.48am on 21 January 1960, while heading the 9.05pm Glasgow St Enoch–St Pancras sleeper, its right-hand coupling rod became disconnected and ploughed into the ballast, just as a down freight was passing, derailing wagons which hit some coaches, resulting in five deaths and eight injured passengers.

No 70052 was new to Polmadie shed (66A) on 21 August 1954, staying for almost eight years until eventually, like nearly all members of the class, it arrived at Carlisle Kingmoor in January 1966. It was withdrawn on 1 April 1967. **Date: 12 March 1966.**

↗ Details of the famous Heaton (Newcastle)–Red Bank (Manchester) empty newspaper van train have already been given on page 128. The attraction of the train was the variety of double-headed locomotive combinations that it produced. On this date, 'Britannia' No 70011 *Hotspur* of Carlisle Upperby shed, minus its front number plate and nameplates, is piloting Class 5 No 44947 of Bolton shed (9K). They are seen just to the west of Heaton Lodge Junction on the Calder Valley main line. No 70011 was withdrawn from Carlisle Kingmoor on 23 December 1967, while No 44947 lasted until 1 July 1968. **Date: 7 May 1966.**

→ Here is another combination of motive power on the Heaton–Red Bank van train. This time we have 'Britannia' No 70018 *Flying Dutchman*, which had just been transferred to Carlisle Upperby (12B), piloting Class B1 4-6-0 No 61030 *Nyala* of Wakefield shed (56A). The train is approaching Brighouse station, which was to close on 5 January 1970 and reopen again 30 years later, on 28 May 2000. No 70018 was yet another 'Britannia' to be withdrawn from Carlisle Kingmoor shed (12A), while No 61030 lasted to the end of steam in West Yorkshire, on 30 September 1967. **Date: 28 May 1966.**

In keeping with the town of Alnwick, the train shed was an imposing building. It opened on 1 October 1850, connecting the town with the East Coast Main Line at Alnmouth, about three miles away. By the date of these pictures it was one of the very few steam-worked passenger services in the North East of England. There was a small shed at Alnmouth, where the branch locomotive was based. Class K1 2-6-0 No 62050 was more than adequate power for the branch. Fortunately, the station building has survived and most of it is now occupied by a well-known second-hand book shop, Barter Books. Over the past 15 years there have been continuous attempts to reopen the branch into Alnwick, but it had not proved possible, owing to buildings having been and about to be constructed on the trackbed, plus the problem of crossing the busy A1 dual carriageway.

However, the Aln Valley Railway has now been granted permission to go ahead with reopening the line from a site alongside the A1, where there is ample parking space, plus room for a museum. Work on the project started in 2012.

Somebody has attached a 10D shedplate indicating Lostock Hall to No 62050, which moved on to North Blyth shed one month after these pictures were taken, where it remained until withdrawn on 9 September 1967.

↖ Picture 1: reversing into the station after running round.
← Picture 2: leaving the station.
↑ Picture 3: inside the station.
Date: 21 May 1966.

⬆ After 12 years allocated to Leeds Holbeck (55A), from 1950 to 1962, 'Jubilee' No 45565 *Victoria* moved to Low Moor shed (56F), where it was kept in fine external condition and used primarily on excursions. These were mainly to Blackpool, although during the week it worked some freight services. It stayed at Low Moor until withdrawn in January 1967, apart for four months at Wakefield (56A). Here, it is seen emerging from behind the signalbox at Low Moor with a train of empty stock heading for Bradford Exchange. Low Moor station closed on 14 June 1965, although there is currently a move to open a new station. The shed was behind the train, which closed when steam ended on the North Eastern Region in September 1967. **Date: 31 May 1966.**

↗ An immaculate No 45565 *Victoria* makes a vigorous departure from Bradford Exchange, past the present site of Bradford Interchange, as it starts to tackle the 1-in-50 gradient to Bowling Junction, with the help of a Fairburn 2-6-4T as a banker. Bradford Exchange opened in 1850 and closed on 14 January 1973, reopening again on the same date, but 200 yards away. It became Bradford Interchange on 16 May 1983 and is still in use. **Date: 21 August 1966.**

→ With a lightweight load of only three coaches, Fairburn 2-6-4T No 42142 did not need any assistance up the 1-in-50 gradient out of Bradford Exchange. It is heading for Wakefield Westgate, with the Bradford portion of an up Leeds to King's Cross express, which will use the Copley Hill triangle to avoid Leeds. This picture was taken from the opposite side of the tracks from the previous view. No 42142 was transferred from the Scottish Region in 1963, and survived at Low Moor until 18 June 1966. **Date: 31 May 1966.**

⬆ By 1966, the Bradford portions of the King's Cross–Leeds trains were normally hauled by Fairburn 2-6-4Ts, but Ivatt 4MT 2-6-0s also appeared occasionally, as is the case on this afternoon, when No 43070 of Wakefield shed arrived at Bradford Exchange. It is descending the 1-in-50 gradient into the station slowly, and behind it is the massive black retaining wall which, when the new station was opened in 1973, was steam cleaned and looked very smart. No 43070 was new in October 1950 but, before withdrawal on 12 August 1967, was transferred 11 times around the North Eastern Region. **Date: 31 May 1966.**

↗ During the mid-1960s, the former Crosti-boilered BR 9F class 2-10-0s became a common sight in West Yorkshire, working oil trains from Stanlow Oil Refinery, across the Pennines to Hunslet oil terminal in Leeds, plus other freight workings. No 92020, seen here passing Bradley Junction to the east of Huddersfield, is on an up mixed freight. The locomotive was the first of the ten Crosti-boilered examples and entered traffic on 18 May 1955, allocated to Wellingborough shed (15A), but they gave a lot of trouble, especially with drifting exhaust and eventually the London Midland Region stored all ten of them.

No 92020 was out of use in April 1959 and did not return to traffic as a conventional-boilered locomotive until June 1961. They were all converted and then gave good service, some of them almost to the end of steam. No 92020 received a light intermediate repair in February 1966 and so was not withdrawn until 21 October 1967. Seven of them were taken out of traffic on 11 November 1967. **Date: 4 June 1966.**

➡ It is hard to believe that, if you stand on this bridge today, all that remains of this once-busy location at Normanton is two through running lines. The shed (55D) can be seen in the background with the coaling tower and several sidings, as Holbeck (55A) Class 5 No 45080 passes with an up freight. The station on the opposite side of the bridge was opened in 1840 and was an important location on the Midland main line, but today, it is nothing more than a bus shelter. No 45080 spent all its career allocated to sheds in the West Riding of Yorkshire which included 18 years at Farnley Junction (55C) until it closed in 1966. The 'Black Five' was withdrawn during the last month of steam in the West Riding, on 9 September 1966. **Date: 2 July 1966.**

The summer Saturdays-only Poole–Bradford Exchange in the 1960s was a favourite with local enthusiasts to travel on, as it was routed from Sheffield via Barnsley–Penistone–Huddersfield–Halifax. This involved the steep climbs from Barnsley to Penistone and from Greetland to Dryclough Junction near Halifax. The regular motive power was a Farnley Junction (55C) 'Jubilee', which always produced a fine sound from the front end up the banks.

The locomotive worked the morning train out, returning in the evening. On this Saturday it was No 45647 *Sturdee*, which is seen crossing Oxspring Viaduct, approaching Penistone, eight miles from Barnsley. **Date: 2 July 1966.**

The former Lancashire & Yorkshire line from Huddersfield met the old Manchester, Sheffield & Lincolnshire Railway line at Penistone. The distance from Huddersfield is only 13 miles and has four major viaducts, as well as several short tunnels. The impressive viaduct at Penistone was designed by Sir John Fowler and carried the railway over the River Don. Completed in 1850, it has 29 arches and is 98ft high, and is a Grade 2 listed structure. These two pictures show the SO Poole–Bradford heading towards Huddersfield with 'Jubilee' No 45647 *Sturdee*, which was withdrawn from Holbeck shed (55C) on 22 April 1967. **Date: 2 July 1966.**

↑ A fine variety of classes is seen inside the roundhouses at York (50A). From left to right: BR Standard 2-6-0 No 77012 of York, Class 5 4-6-0 No 45363 of Carlisle Kingmoor, BR Standard 9F 2-10-0 No 92206 of York, preserved A4 class No 60019 *Bittern*, and local Class V2 2-6-2 No 60831. This had been allocated here since 1959, having spent several years on the ex-Great Central line, and was the last V2 to be withdrawn from York shed, on 3 December 1966. **Date: 12 December 1966.**

↓ This is a rather depressing sight at the Leeds end of Neville Hill Yard, showing Class A4 No 60010 *Dominion of Canada* being hauled by BR Standard 4-6-0 No 75019 from Darlington Works, en route to Crewe Works for a cosmetic overhaul. It was handed over to the Canadian High Commissioner on 10 April 1967 and loaded aboard MV *Beaveroak* at the Royal Victoria Dock, London and departed for its new home at the Canadian Railway Museum at Delson/Saint Constant, about 15 miles from the port Montreal. It is now (October 2012) back in this country to take part in a line-up of all existing Class A4s during 2013. **Date: 27 April 1966.**

↑ A Locomotive Club of Great Britain railtour visited the Gosport branch, which lost its passenger services on 8 June 1953, but remained open for freight until 1969. Using a Bulleid Q1 class 0-6-0, No 33006, the tour then made its way to Southampton Terminus, where it handed over to two USA class 0-6-0Ts, Nos 30064 and 30073, both in lined-green livery. The passengers took the opportunity to get out and take some pictures, as one did in those days, although it had been established that the special was the only train using the station during the day. The station was due to close six months later, on 5 September 1966. The tour then proceeded down the Fawley branch. **Date: 19 March 1966.**

→ The following day, the Railway Correspondence & Travel Society ran another tour along the Fawley branch, using the same USA 0-6-0Ts as the previous day, only this time they were coupled bunker to bunker. The pair is seen passing Marchwood, which had lost its passenger services one month earlier, the same day as Fawley. No 30064 passed into preservation at the Bluebell Railway, while No 30073 was withdrawn on 12 December 1966 and scrapped. **Date: 20 March 1966.**

⬆ Parkstone bank is about 2½ miles long and starts just to the east of Poole station and goes as far as Branksome with some parts at 1 in 60. Very often, heavy Southern Region trains were banked up the hill. Parkstone station was halfway up the bank, so restarting, especially with 'unrebuilt' Bulleid Pacifics, could be difficult in adverse conditions. 'Battle of Britain' No 34066 *Spitfire* has the help of a banker as it restarts a Saturdays-only Poole–Newcastle away from Parkstone station. *Spitfire* entered traffic on 5 September 1947 as No 21C166 and was allocated to Ramsgate shed (74B), moving to Stewarts Lane (73A) in December 1949, and stayed until February 1961.

During this period, it was involved in the terrible Lewisham disaster in fog, when it was hauling the 4.56pm Cannon Street to Ramsgate express and ran into the rear of a stationary suburban electric under the Lewisham–Nunhead flyover, resulting in the flyover buckling and collapsing on to the three rear coaches of the EMU. This resulted in 90 deaths and 173 injuries. *Spitfire* spent five weeks being repaired and re-entered service on 22 March 1958. It was never rebuilt and was eventually withdrawn on 10 September 1966, having only covered 652,908 miles in 19 years of service, according to the records. **Date: 29 July 1966.**

↗ This picture shows what a terrible external state most of the Bulleid Pacifics and other locomotives on the Southern Region had got into by 1966. Judging by the amount of ash lying around the shed, conditions, at Bournemouth at least, were just as bad. No 34023 *Blackmore Vale*, along with No 34102 *Lapford*, became the last of the 'unrebuilt' 'West Countries', both being withdrawn on 9 September 1967. Only two of the 'unrebuilt' examples achieved 1 million miles in service, with *Blackmore Vale* managing 921,268 miles in 21 years of service. It passed into preservation and is based on the Bluebell Railway. **Date: 20 March 1966.**

➡ Another view in the yard of Bournemouth shed (71B) is showing rebuilt 'West Country' No 34032 *Camelford*, in reasonably clean condition, because it was allocated to Salisbury shed (72B), which must have had some cleaners at the time. In the background is No 34021 *Dartmoor*. New, as No 21C132 in June 1946, *Camelford* was an Eastern Division locomotive until March 1950, when it moved to the West Country. It was rebuilt as late as October 1960, but its end came on 2 October 1966, only having covered 204,243 miles as a rebuild, and it was sent for scrapping to Buttigieg's yard at Newport. **Date: 20 March 1966.**

↑ In the days when my local station at Mirfield had a roof and a waiting room with a fire burning in it during winter, compared to the current terrible bus shelters, it sees the arrival of the Leeds–Wavertree van train with Holbeck 'Jubilee' No 45593 *Kolhapur*. It had been specially cleaned for the duty, as Patrick Whitehouse was travelling on the footplate, prior to him eventually buying it for preservation. The 4-6-0 was built by the North British Locomotive Co Ltd in 1934, and was allocated mainly to West Coast sheds during its career, arriving at Holbeck in April 1965.

Together with No 45562 *Alberta*, it was used regularly on the summer Saturday extras on the Settle & Carlisle, as well as on railtours. It was withdrawn when steam finished in the West Riding, in September 1967. **Date: 19 September 1966.**

↖ BR Class 4MT, 4-6-0 No 75070 emerges from under the roof of Bournemouth station and heads for the shed for servicing. This fine station was opened in 1885 and was known as Bournemouth Central from 1899, but 'Central' was dropped in 1967. No 75070 was based at Eastleigh shed (71A) and was attached to a BR1B-type tender, giving it a capacity of 4,725 gallons of water. It was also fitted with a double chimney, as were all the Southern Region members of the class. At the date of this picture it only had another six weeks left in service, being withdrawn in September 1966. **Date: 22 July 1966.**

← The use of 'Austerity' 2-8-0s on railtours was rare, but the Locomotive Club of Great Britain used No 90076 for part of a tour, which came across the Pennines to Yorkshire. It travelled via Halifax and took the triangle at Low Moor, and ran down the Cleckheaton branch to Wakefield. No 90076 took over from 'Crab' 2-6-0 No 42942 for a trip to Goole, where it is seen at the station. No 90076 served in Belgium during the Second World War and was purchased by the LNER, becoming Class O7 No 3076. It lasted virtually to the end of steam in the North Eastern Region, spending eight years at Wakefield shed (56A), from 1959 to 1967, and was withdrawn on 9 September 1967. **Date: 8 October 1966.**

↑ On a superb crisp winter's morning, the Locomotive Club of Great Britain ran a special over Copy Pit with Holbeck 'Jubilee' No 45593 *Kolhapur*. It is seen climbing towards the summit past Portsmouth, Yorkshire, that once had a station, but which closed on 7 July 1958. The tour was heading to what is now the East Lancashire Railway, but went through to Bacup, as services were being withdrawn on that day. Details of No 45593 are on page 163. **Date: 3 December 1966.**

↖ On another crisp winter's morning Class 8F 2-8-0 No 48394 heads a down freight past Belle Busk, which is detailed on page 143. No 48394 had been allocated to West Yorkshire since Nationalisation and was at Stourton shed (55B) at the time of this picture. It was withdrawn on 20 May 1967. **Date: 15 January 1966.**

← Manningham-allocated (55F) Ivatt 4MT 2-6-0 No 43074 is on local duties, shunting the yard at Idle on the Laisterdyke to Shipley line. Idle was opened in April 1875, but lost its passenger services in February 1931, but remained open for freight until 5 October 1968. No 43074 was withdrawn on 18 June 1966 after spending 4½ years at Bradford Manningham. **Date: 15 January 1966.**

1967

As the new year arrived, it became clear that it would be the last year for main line steam in any quantity on BR. There were six months left to enjoy some fantastic performances being put up by the crews and the Bulleid Pacifics on the Waterloo–Bournemouth expresses. The railway must have made a fair bit of money from those who travelled frequently, but the electrification was getting nearer to completion and 2 July was set as the official 'farewell to steam' day on the Southern, but actual steam operation on the region was extended for a further week until the 9th.

Two specials were run from Waterloo. The first was to Weymouth behind 'Merchant Navy' No 35008 *Orient Line* with 11 coaches, which returned double headed to Bournemouth with No 35007 *Aberdeen Commonwealth*. The other ran to Bournemouth and return with No 35028 *Clan Line*. Far fewer enthusiasts travelled than had been expected, owing to the high cost and also, most of them knew that on a high-profile occasion, they were not going to get a performance with 100mph, like some had achieved on the service trains.

The 'Pines Express' ran for the last time on 4 March but it passed almost unnoticed, as two Brush Type 4 diesels worked the trains.

It was a bad year for the railways, particularly the Southern Region, as there were some serious accidents. On 5 November, between Grove Park and Hither Green, a 12-coach EMU was derailed at 70mph because of a broken rail, causing the train to split. The rear portion slewed across the tracks, resulting in the deaths of 49 passengers with 78 injured. Another accident happened at Raynes Park, which caused the deaths of 13 people and 61 injured. Much further north, prototype diesel-electric No DP2 came to a premature end when it hit some derailed wagons near Thirsk, while travelling north on the East Coast Main Line.

By the end of the year, all the 'Britannias' had been withdrawn, except for No 70013 *Oliver Cromwell*, which was well occupied on railtour duties. By this time, most specials were hauled by BR Standard 5MT 4-6-0s, ex-LMS Stanier Class 5s and occasionally Stanier 8F 2-8-0s. The last remaining Southern Region engines all went in July.

The line closures had slowed down in 1967, but included the following, which were lost:

Bodmin Road–Bodmin and Wadebridge–Padstow 30 January	March–St Ives 6 March
Sidmouth Junction–Sidmouth–Exmouth 6 March	Manchester Central–Cheadle Heath 6 March
Three Bridges–Tunbridge Wells 2 January	Millers Dale–Buxton 6 March
Appledore–New Romney 6 March	Northallerton–Harrogate 6 March
Cambridge–Sudbury via Long Melford 6 March	Kinnaber Junction–Stanley Junction via Forfar 4 September
	Hillington West–Renfrew Wharf 5 June

Other withdrawals included the Tyneside electrics after 30 years' service, as well as all five North British Type 4 D600 series 'Warship' diesel-hydraulics. The English Electric Type 4 (later Class 50) started to appear, which developed such a large following in later years. There were also several new designs of freight wagons entering service.

The preservation movement really got going, with all sorts of schemes surfacing to preserve locomotives, with some successes.

The last steam engine to be withdrawn from the Eastern Region was K1 class No 62005, except for two carriage-heating B1 class 4-6-0s at Sheffield Nunnery carriage sidings, which were allowed to travel at reduced speed to Normanton for coaling. The last steam-hauled revenue-earning working on the Eastern Region (now merged with the North Eastern Region) was the 15.00 freight from Carlton Sidings to Goole, hauled by Stanier 8F No 48276 which returned light engine to Royston shed.

The last BR shunting horse was withdrawn from service at Newmarket, after being allocated there for 18 years. No preservation offer was forthcoming, so 'Charlie' was transferred to green pastures in Somerset, where he died on 29 October 1968 aged 29, rendering another BR class extinct.

⬆ BR 9F 2-10-0 No 92211, transferred to Wakefield shed (56A) in November 1966, appears to be struggling with this up freight while climbing the 1-in-105 gradient from Huddersfield to Marsden as it passes over Milnsbridge Viaduct. This was in the days when there were four tracks all the way from Heaton Lodge Junction to Marsden and through Standedge Tunnels and beyond. No 92211 only managed 7 years 8 months in service, from September 1959 to being condemned on 22 May 1967. However, it managed to be allocated to the Western, Southern and North Eastern regions during its short working career. **Date: 8 February 1967.**

⬇ Several enthusiasts had spent the night cleaning BR 4MT 4-6-0 No 75048 ready for the morning up 'Cambrian Coast Express', and they had done a fine job. Blessed with a fine winter's morning, the train's schedule made it very easy to follow and photograph all the way to Welshpool, so several decent pictures were obtained. When the London Midland Region took over the Cambrian lines in September 1963, it was quick to replace the ex-Great Western locomotives with BR Standard 4MT 75000 and 76000 classes, plus some 82000 series 2-6-2Ts. No 75048 was allocated to Croes Newydd shed (6C) in May 1966 and remained there until steam finished on the Cambrian lines. Eventually, it was allocated to Carnforth (24L) and remained in service to the end of steam in August 1968. **Date: 11 February 1967.**

⬆ The Cambrian line between Borth and Machynlleth is virtually level and the well-cleaned No 75048 is making good progress between Dovey Junction and Machynlleth with the up 'Cambrian Coast Express'. **Date: 11 February 1967.**

↑ One mile east of Machynlleth the gradient profile of the Cambrian line alters dramatically. There is a 12½-mile climb with just a half-mile stretch of level track at Llanbrynmair, after 9 miles of continuous climbing before a final 3½ miles of 1 in 52/56 to the summit at Talerddig. The decent down the other side through Carno and Caersws is far less severe and No 75048 is shown passing Llanbrynmair, taking advantage of the half-mile of level track. **Date: 11 February 1967.**

→ No 75048 emerges from the deep cutting almost at Talerddig Summit. **Date: 11 February 1967.**

It has been easy going and quite fast from Talerddig Summit 14 miles away, as No 75048 arrives at Newtown station. It was the second site for the station which opened in June 1861, and is still in use today. **Date: 11 February 1967.**

◄ March 4 1967 not only marked the end of steam on the Cambrian lines but also the end of the 'Cambrian Coast Express'. The train was introduced on 15 July 1927, but was withdrawn during the Second World War. It was reintroduced on 7 July 1951, but only ran on summer Saturdays until 1953. From 1954 onwards, it ran Mondays to Saturdays, with a portion for Pwllheli, although in 1966, this was replaced by a DMU connection at Dovey Junction. The headboard was the last to be used by the Western Region.

The train was notable for two main reasons. In the 1950s and early 1960s, it was the longest steam diagram for crews and locomotives at Old Oak Common shed, and it was always allocated one of the best 'Kings' or 'Castles' for the return trip to Shrewsbury. Aberystwyth shed always kept the 'Manors' used on this train in immaculate condition. By 1967, the 'Manors' had long since gone and the BR 4MT 4-6-0s had taken over. No 75033 is seen doing the honours on the last day, complete with headboard, where it is ready to leave Aberystwyth station for the last time. Little was done to mark the return working from Shrewsbury, which was hauled by a very dirty, double-chimney No 75006. **Date: 4 March 1967.**

↑ Sunday 5 February, unexpectedly, turned out to be rather a special day on the Settle & Carlisle, as it was the last time steam was used to haul a procession of specials (apart from enthusiast trips) over the line. Wales had been playing Scotland at Murrayfield and the rugby faithful had headed north in their thousands. I have no idea about the result but, when information leaked out that the five returning specials were all to be worked by 'Britannias' over the S&C, I, along with many others, suddenly became very interested in the event.

I duly presented myself at Ais Gill Summit at the appointed time, to see No 70014 head south. I moved to Kirkby Stephen to see No 70039 and followed it to the summit, got No 70003 on Mallerstang Common, then ignored a Class 47 diesel, which had filled in for No 70002, and waited for No 70010 on the last train. The weather was not good but at least the sun came out as 70010 passed Kirkby Stephen, which is shown in this picture. I am sure there were enough diesels around Carlisle to cover the workings, but somebody at Kingmoor shed had pulled a few strings in the right places. **Date: 5 February 1967.**

To mark the end of through services between Paddington and Birkenhead, two specials were run, organised by Ian Allan Ltd. The first, the 'Birkenhead Flyer', was hauled to Chester by preserved 'Castle' No 4079 *Pendennis Castle* and the second, named 'The Zulu', by No 7029 *Clun Castle*. Birkenhead-allocated BR 9F 2-10-0s hauled the trains from Chester to Birkenhead. There was also a Stephenson Locomotive Society special running. No 7029 *Clun Castle* is seen leaving Wrexham on the return journey. **Date: 5 March 1967.**

Stops were made by the specials on the return journeys from Birkenhead at Hooton for the passengers to take photographs, producing this incredible sight. The 9F is No 92203 built in 1959 and withdrawn on 9 December 1967, which by July 1962 had only covered 91,434 miles. Fortunately, it was bought by David Sheppard and passed into preservation. The other 9F involved was No 92234, new in August 1958 and withdrawn on 11 November 1967 with only 93,949 miles recorded to the end of 1962. In addition to the specials, normal service trains were running. **Date: 5 March 1967.**

↑ On my last visit to Bournemouth shed (71B), 'Merchant Navy' No 35013 *Blue Funnel* was blowing off outside. It was new in February 1945 as No 21C13 and was allocated to Nine Elms (70A) for the first nine years and then had ten years at Exmouth Junction (72A). During this period it was rebuilt in 1956. In the last few months of steam on the Southern Region most speed restrictions on the Bournemouth line had been lifted and some remarkable performances were achieved by the crews.

Apparently, No 35013 was one of the best performers and attained 106mph on 26 June, only a few days before withdrawal, but even more remarkable had been its performance on 28 April when it left Waterloo 14 minutes late with 12 coaches and a van, and arrived at Winchester one minute early, with 104mph being achieved. It was withdrawn in July 1967 after having run 1,114,658 miles, according to records, and was eventually scrapped at Buttigieg's at Newport in October. **Date: 23 June 1967.**

↑ Looking well cleaned although it was just over a month from withdrawal, 'Jubilee' No 45647 *Sturdee* is passing Coniston Cold, halfway between Skipton and Hellifield, with an afternoon Leeds–Heysham van train. The 4-6-0's last six months were allocated to Holbeck (55A), having spent 28 years working from West Coast Main Line sheds. It had a heavy general repair in 1961, which accounted for it lasting almost to the end of steam in West Yorkshire, and the records state that it travelled 1,293,844 miles to the end of 1960, so it probably achieved well over 1.5 million miles in total. **Date: 18 March 1967.**

↖ ← In the days when there was relatively little traffic along the Aire Valley roads, at least compared with today's standards, and onwards to Blea Moor, one was able to follow freight trains fairly easily. The 12.55 from Stourton to Carlisle was usually a 'Britannia' or a 9F 2-10-0 in 1967, but on this occasion Holbeck 'Jubilee' No 45697 *Achilles* was in charge. I once obtained 22 shots of this train between the outskirts of Leeds and Blea Moor, but on this day only went as far as Skipton. It is seen passing Newlay, four miles north of Leeds travelling on the down fast line when there were four tracks to Shipley. The second picture shows it pulling out of the loop at Skipton South after a crew change. Note that the locomotive is attached to a lined-black tender from a Class 5. Details of No 45697 are on page 143. **Date: 15 March 1967.**

⬆ The 12.55 Stourton–Carlisle freight received plenty of attention in 1967 as it was a regular runner with interesting motive power, as mentioned previously, and also because the sun was in the correct position for most locations. Class 9F No 92110 appeared on the train on this day and is seen entering the cutting between Newlay and Calverley, to the north of Leeds. This was once a fine photographic section of line until electrification came to the Aire Valley. Locomotive details are on the previous page. **Date: 23 June 1967.**

◰ Just occasionally, one happens to be in the right position at the right time, as was the case when I managed to get 9F 2-10-0 No 92110 heading south on the up Long Meg anhydrite train as 'Britannia' No 70029 (formerly *Shooting Star*) was climbing the 'Long Drag' on the Settle & Carlisle past Stainforth Sidings just north of Settle, on the 12.55pm Stourton–Carlisle freight. No 70029 was the last of the five allocated new to Cardiff Canton (86C) in October 1952 for working the expresses to Paddington.

Unlike the rest of the Western Region crews, the Canton men seemed to get on well with the class and they were kept in immaculate condition. In September 1961, they were transferred to the London Midland Region where they remained until withdrawn, most from Carlisle Kingmoor shed, No 70029 lasting until September 1967. Class 9F No 92110 spent the last two years of its 11-year career allocated to Carlisle Kingmoor (12A) before being withdrawn on 30 December 1967, when the shed closed. **Date: 18 April 1967.**

◰ The Stanlow–Leeds Hunslet oil trains continued until steam finished in West Yorkshire, in September 1967, and were worked almost entirely by BR 9F 2-10-0s including the ex-Crosti boiler locomotives. No 92024, without a front number plate, is pulling away from Neville Hill yard where the train had reversed after coming up the branch from Hunslet. Notice the barrier wagons behind the locomotive. No 92024 was new in 1955 and had three years as a Crosti before being converted in June 1958. It had a light repair at Crewe in 1965 and continued in traffic until 11 November 1967. **Date: 14 April 1967.**

◄ Out of the 842 Stanier Class 5 4-6-0s, No 44767 was unique. It was built at Crewe Works in 1947 with outside Stephenson link motion, double blastpipe and chimney, Timken roller bearings, and electric lighting. The double blastpipe and chimney and electric lighting were removed and it remained in service until almost the end of steam at Carlisle Kingmoor shed, after which it passed into preservation. A close-up of the motion is seen inside Holbeck shed at Leeds (55A). **Date: 15 June 1967.**

↑An unofficial transfer of No 44767 took place around April/May, from Kingmoor (12A) to Holbeck (55A) as the district motive power superintendent was keen to find out more about No 44767 and how it compared with the other Class 5s. I never found out what conclusions were drawn, but I do know that the engine was highly rated by the crews I talked to occasionally, when it was allocated to Bank Hall shed at Liverpool (27A) for working the Calder Valley expresses. Another view of the 12.55pm Stourton–Carlisle freight, entering Newlay cutting with No 44767. **Date: 14 June 1967.**

⬆ Storm clouds are gathering over Tebay as 'Britannia' No 70021 (formally named *Morning Star*) climbs Shap past Greenholme on the 9.10 Rugby to Glasgow parcels, but without a banker. No 70021 had only been allocated to Kingmoor shed (12A) three months before this picture was taken, but was withdrawn when the shed closed on 31 December 1967. It was new in August 1951 and it spent almost 5½ years at Plymouth Laira (83D) which was no doubt pleased to see it transferred to Cardiff Canton (86C) in January 1957. It moved to the London Midland Region on 13 July 1958, to Trafford Park (9E) to work the Manchester Central–St Pancras expresses. **Date: 25 September 1967.**

◤ A very rare view, and possibly the only time a 'Britannia' Pacific ever worked between Huddersfield and Penistone in BR Steam days, No 70013 *Oliver Cromwell* was in charge of this special from Lancashire. It travelled via the Calder Valley main line and took the Bradley triangle to head for Huddersfield and on to Penistone and Sheffield. It is approaching Penistone Viaduct before arriving at the station. **Date: 28 October 1967.**

◤ This picture was taken at Manningham shed (55F) of 'Britannia' No 70034 (formally named *Thomas Hardy*) waiting to haul the 19.40 Valley Road (Bradford) freight to Carlisle. It is in unlined-green livery but it has been attached to a B1D-type tender as originally fitted to the last ten members of the class, Nos 70045 to 70054. By this date it only had another five weeks in service before being withdrawn on 6 May 1967 and scrapped at McWilliams at Shettleston. It was new in December 1952 and had six months at Longsight shed (9A) before being transferred to Stewarts Lane on the Southern Region where it only stayed one month before moving to Stratford (30A) to work the East Anglian expresses out of Liverpool Street. **Date: 21 March 1967.**

↑ Stanier 8F No 48168 of Heaton Mersey shed (9F) passing Bradley Junction to the east of Huddersfield, when there were four tracks. It is working an additional tank train back over the Pennines probably to Stanlow, which at this time would normally have had a BR 9F 2-10-0. Bradley Junction was the Huddersfield end of the triangle between Heaton Lodge Junction and Bradley Wood Junction, which is now again in use after being closed for several years. No 48168 lasted in service until 1 July 1968. **Date: 18 October 1967.**

↗ The freight on the Grassington branch from Skipton had been in the hands of Midland 4F 0-6-0s for decades, until the mid-1960s when the BR 4MT class 4-6-0s took over and were allocated to Skipton shed. No 75020 is seen climbing the ten-mile branch with traffic for Swinden Quarry and Grassington. Passenger services had ceased in the 1930s, but the line still remains open for limestone traffic from the quarry. No 75020 was one of the nine Western Region members of the class that received a double chimney and was painted in lined-green livery. It entered service in November 1953 and was withdrawn in August 1968. It spent a period in store in 1966 and 1967 and was one of eight of the class to be overhauled at Cowlairs Works in Glasgow. **Date: 13 June 1967.**

→ In the week before the end of steam on the North Eastern Region, Low Moor shed was full of locos which had steamed for the last time. Fairburn 2-6-4T No 42141 is in steam with B1 4-6-0 No 61337. Other Fairburns, Nos 42152 and 42251, are also seen. **Date: 23 September 1967.**

↑ Ex-Crosti 9F No 92022 has only another three months left in service from Speke Junction shed (8C). It is climbing very slowly past Linthwaite, allowing many pictures to be taken up the 1-in-105 gradient from Huddersfield to Marsden, with a mixed freight on the up fast, in the days of four tracks. It was new in May 1955 and nearly managed two years as a Crosti locomotive, before being stored and sent to Crewe Works to be converted into a conventional locomotive. **Date: 8 July 1967.**

↗ During the mid-1960s, Low Moor shed became adept at holding on to good engines that had been loaned for a weekend for summer Saturday extras. BR Standard 5MT Caprotti No 73141 was an example, from Patricroft shed, when it stayed around for at least a couple of weeks. These locomotives were usually diagrammed for the Saturdays-only Bradford Exchange to Bridlington and return which, by this date, had become the longest steam diagram in the country. No 73141 was one of the batch built between October and December 1956, allocated to the Midland main line sheds for working to St Pancras, but by this time, like many members of the class, it had been re-allocated to Patricroft shed (9H) in 1964. Here, it is seen climbing the 1 in 50 out of Bradford Exchange past Hall Lane, with the help of a banker, to Bowling Junction at the top of the bank, on the SO Bridlington working. The 4-6-0 was withdrawn two weeks after this picture was taken. **Date: 1 July 1967.**

→ It was unusual for trains to be double headed out of Bradford Exchange, except when Type 2 diesels were attached around this period for crew training. Two Fairburn 2-6-4T tanks are climbing the 1 in 50 past Hall Lane and are heading for Laisterdyke. They will leave the ex-Lancashire & Yorkshire line at St Dunstans, where there was a station which closed in September 1952. The locomotives are Nos 42066 and 42073, both having entered service on the Southern Region, but were at Low Moor (56F) at this date. No 42066 had only been allocated three weeks previously but was withdrawn three months later in August, while No 42073 had been in the area for some time and lasted until 9 September, before passing into preservation. Unfortunately, I did not record where the train was going. **Date: 29 May 1967.**

⬆ Wold Fell stands out on the horizon as ex-Crosti-boilered BR 9F No 92021 approaches Dent with a down freight on the Settle & Carlisle line. It entered service in May 1955 and was converted to a normal boiler in June 1960, having achieved a very low annual mileage of around 18,000 to 20,000 during this time. It had a light intermediate repair in February 1966 and lasted in service until 11 November, allocated to Birkenhead shed (6C). Its progress up the 'Long Drag' on this Saturday afternoon was very slow and made it easy to follow. **Date: 5 August 1967.**

↗ Undoubtedly, the most unexpected event on the railways in Yorkshire in 1967, was the allocation of 'Jubilee' No 45562 *Alberta*, to haul the Royal Train on 30 May 1967. Prince Philip was travelling to Nidd Bridge on the Harrogate to Ripon line, which had lost its passenger services in March, but remained open for freight as far as Ripon. Nidd Bridge closed completely in 1964. Class 5 No 45428 was the standby locomotive and both were turned out in spotless condition. The authority for this must have come from the District Motive Power Superintendent, who was known to be a steam enthusiast and who was responsible for keeping the Holbeck 'Jubilees' working over the Settle & Carlisle in 1966 and 1967, plus much unofficial help to the preservation movement.

The train is seen at Wormald Green, running empty stock in order to reverse and turn at Ripon. There was an unconfirmed report that, when Prince Philip asked the driver what type of engine *Alberta* was, he replied tactfully that it was a 'Sandringham'. **Date: 30 May 1967.**

➡ The Stephenson Locomotive Society ran a special, 1Z15, which was electric hauled to Stockport, where 'Britannia' No 70038 *Robin Hood* (painted name), well cleaned and in unlined-green livery, took over for a trip to York via Standedge and return. The special is seen just to the west of Bradley Junction, which is east of Huddersfield, in the evening sunshine. Its performance on the 1-in-105 climb to Marsden was not brilliant, allowing several pictures to be taken. In spite of its appearance, it was withdrawn five weeks after the tour, on 12 August 1967. **Date: 2 July 1967.**

↑ Two days before the end of steam at Holbeck shed, 'Jubilee' No 45593 *Kolhapur* is at the entrance to the roundhouse. Details about *Kolhapur* are given on pages 163 and 165. **Date: 29 September 1967.**

↗ On the last day of steam services in the Bradford/Leeds area, Holbeck Class 5 No 45428 is suitably inscribed on the smokebox, as it prepares to leave Bradford Exchange on its last duty back to Leeds, on a King's Cross train. The very last steam service to leave Bradford Exchange was the 16.18 to King's Cross, hauled by Fairburn 2-6-4T No 42152.

No 45428 was stored in the roundhouses at Holbeck and became the last steam engine to leave the shed, on 24 August 1968, when it went in steam to Tyseley for preservation. **Date: 1 October 1967.**

→ Six weeks after closure, the autumn sun shines inside Holbeck shed (55A), on the smokebox of Class 5 No 45428 as it waits for the next phase of its career in preservation. It was a very odd experience for me, wandering around in the silent roundhouses, still with immaculate locomotives around the turntables but without the smell of smoke and all the familiar noises that steam engines made on shed. After the locomotives had departed, the demolition men moved in during 1969 and the roundhouses, plus the massive coaling bunkers, were brought down, and so 99 years as an active steam shed passed into history. A new chapter then opened, when a diesel maintenance depot began operations. **Date: 8 November 1967.**

1968

During the early part of the year I hardly did any photography. Much of the action was around the Chinley and Peak Forrest area, with Stanier 8Fs. From March onwards the 'last' specials started running with nearly all of them operating on routes within 40 miles of Manchester. As the months passed, using fewer and fewer lines, a rough estimate suggests there were about 58 specials run in 1968, up to and including 11 August, of which only 32 had steam haulage for part of the journey.

Details of the last day of regular steam operation, together with the six specials operated on 4 August are given in the picture captions but, as it is said, as one door closes another one opens. So it was in the Yorkshire area, as the Keighley & Worth Valley Railway ran the opening special on 29 June, headed by red-liveried Ivatt 2-6-2T No 41241 and USA 0-6-0T No 72 in a brown livery. This of course provided some replacement at least, of the end of BR steam for the local enthusiasts.

Closures continued at a very much reduced rate with specials for minor lines now being in the hands of DMUs. Closures which took place in 1968 included the following:

Okehampton–Bere Alston 6 May
Hailsham–Polegate 9 September
King's Lynn–Dereham 9 September
March–Magdalen Road via Wisbech
  9 September
Bicester–Bletchley 1 January
Bedford St Johns–Cambridge 1 January
Stratford upon Avon–Cheltenham 25 March
Matlock–Chinley 1 July

Penarth–Cadoxton via Lavernock 6 May
Alnmouth–Alnwick 30 January
Falkirk–Grangemouth 29 January
Larbert–Alloa 29 January
Craigellachie–Elgin 6 May
Craigellachie–Keith 6 May
Elgin–Cairnie Junction via Cullen 6 May
Ayr–Heads of Ayr 16 September
Dunfermline Upper–Stirling 7 October

There were, of course, some more closures to come later on in the 1970s.

After 11 August the only steam locomotives operated by BR were the three on the narrow gauge Vale of Rheidol Railway in Mid-Wales. On the national network, steam locomotives vanished from the news but there were a few events worth a mention.

The 4,000hp *Kestrel* diesel-electric left Brush's works on 20 January for Derby, and went for trials between Shirebrook and Whitemoor. The first of the 'Baby Deltics' were withdrawn, and the new Euston station was opened by HM the Queen.

There was the terrible Hixon disaster on 6 January, when the 11.30 Manchester–Euston hit a 120-ton transformer at a level crossing, killing three people in the cab of the electric loco, and eight passengers. Another 44 people were also badly injured.

On the preservation side there was plenty of positive activity. The Bluebell Railway purchased the freehold of the line between Sheffield Park and Horsted Keynes from BR. The Ffestiniog Railway opened its extension to Dduallt on 19 June, and the Longmoor Military Railway became the home of Bulleid Pacifics *Clan Line* and *Blackmore Vale* and other privately owned preserved locomotives.

The Isle of Wight Steam Railway purchased Class O2 0-4-4T No 24 *Calbourne* and 'Jubilee' No 5596 *Bahamas* was overhauled at the Hunslet Engine Co, Leeds. The North Eastern Locomotive Preservation Group (NELPG) bought Class J27 0-6-0 No 65894 and Q6 0-8-0 No 63395, while the North Yorkshire Moors Railway started negotiations for the purchase of the Pickering to Grosmont line.

This was all excellent news, but for me, not a substitute for the real thing. I turned my attentions abroad and visited Spain, Germany and Portugal, which was the real start of many railway holidays around the world.

⬆ Buxworth curve, just to the north of Chinley station, is an impressive location, especially back in the days of four tracks. The climb for up trains, from Cheadle Heath to the summit at Peak Forest, was just over 16 miles with the gradient as steep as 1 in 90. Buxworth is on the 1-in-90 gradient and the crew of 'Britannia' No 70013 *Oliver Cromwell* put on a splendid display for the assembled crowd of photographers. The special was the 'Midland Main Line Centenary Special', which on the outward journey from St Pancras to Manchester Victoria, travelled via Matlock and Millers Dale and was the last steam passenger train to travel over this section of the main line, as it closed on 1 July 1968. *Oliver Cromwell* hauled the special on the return from Manchester Victoria back to Nottingham, travelling via the Hope Valley route. A Class 45 'Peak' diesel then took over to St Pancras. **Date: 9 June 1968.**

⬆ A final picture on the Grassington branch of BR Standard 4MT No 75019 shows it emerging from Haw Bank Tunnel on the outskirts of Skipton, blowing off as it drifts down the bank. No 75019 was new to Southport shed (27C) in 1952, and spent all its time allocated to sheds in the North West area, eventually being withdrawn from Carnforth on 4 August 1968. **Date: 1 June 1968.**

◥ The early morning stone train to Swinden Quarry on the Grassington branch became one of the last regular steam-hauled freight trains in the area, and developed quite a following of photographers. On most mornings, they would get their pictures and then rush back to their places of work, usually arriving a little late, giving all sorts of unlikely excuses other than they had been photographing a steam train.

   The BR 4MT 4-6-0s were the regular motive power, with No 75019 being the most frequently used and which was kept well cleaned by the enthusiasts. Here, it is shown leaving the quarry, blowing off and giving a good exhaust, which had all been prearranged. **Date: 1 June 1968.**

◀ It came as a surprise to find that BR 4MT 4-6-0 No 75019 had been diagrammed to work the morning stone train from Swinden Quarry right through to Appleby. This turned out to be the last steam-hauled freight over the Settle & Carlisle under British Railways. The locomotive tackled the 'Long Drag' at a steady but fairly slow pace, and with an extremely co-operative crew, who entered into the spirit of the occasion, allowing plenty of pictures to be obtained. The last one that I took is shown here of the train approaching Ribblehead station. **Date: 31 May 1968.**

Two pictures of a very comprehensive tour, within approximately a 30-mile radius of Manchester, was run by Mersey Rail Travel and the Severn Valley Railway Society, and named the 'North West Tour'. It arrived at Stockport from Birmingham behind an electric, where Class 5s Nos 45110 and 44949 took over. It then headed for Disley, Buxton and Peak Forest. It is seen just outside Buxton heading to Chinley, where the second picture of it was taken leaving for Stalybridge. Here, BR Standard 5MTs Nos 73134 and 73069 took over, heading over Standedge and up the Calder Valley line, over Copy Pit and via Blackburn to Bolton. Class 8F No 48773 then headed it to Rochdale, Oldham, Philips Park and back to Stockport. Finally, 9F No 92160 hauled the train to Liverpool. It was an excellent day out with a good variety of locomotives. **Date: 20 April 1968.**

⬆ The state of the ash pits at Rose Grove shed (10F) and the external state of the locomotive suggests that the message has got through that the end of steam is fast approaching. Class 8F No 48257 is awaiting attention. **Date: 17 February 1968.**

⬆ For decades, the banking of coal trains from Stansfield Hall Junction to Copy Pit had been the main feature of this four-mile climb, which was as steep as 1-in-65. A coal train from West Yorkshire, headed by Stanier 8F No 48410 is being banked by classmate No 48519, which is seen passing the signalbox at Portsmouth, where the gradient has eased to 1 in 80. No 48519 survived at Rose Grove (10F) until steam ended. **Date: 18 May 1968.**

◤ Other than steam specials, there were few steam workings on Saturday afternoons by June 1968, although this Colne to Red Bank (Manchester) van train was usually steam hauled. Enthusiasts had only had enough time to clean the smokebox of 2-8-0 No 48257 before it left Rose Grove shed. It is seen just out of the shed with the coaling tower on the skyline. **Date: 1 June 1968.**

◀ A few miles further down the line from the previous picture is Church & Oswaldwistle station, where No 48257 is seen passing with the Colne–Red Bank vans. No 48257 was another 8F to survive to the end of steam. **Date: 1 June 1968.**

◤ With another six months to go before the end of steam, Stanier 8F No 48384 is on the ash pits at Rose Grove shed, awaiting attention, dwarfed by the coaling bunker. No 48384 was running with a lined-out tender from a withdrawn Class 5 at this time. The 2-8-0 was withdrawn on 18 May 1968. **Date: 17 February 1968.**

◄ The sun is setting at Rose Grove shed, with two days to go before closure, as three 8Fs, Nos 48448, 48062 and 48666, await their last trip to the breaker's yard, with the cooling towers of Huncote Power Station in the distance. **Date: 2 August 1968.**

↑ A silhouette of 8F No 48081, dumped and withdrawn at Rose Grove (10F), which was awaiting its final journey. It had been withdrawn on 24 February 1968. **Date: 10 June 1968.**

⬆ The Manchester Rail & Travel Society, with the Severn Valley Railway Society, ran the 'Farewell to BR Steam' special, with every different class that was still running. It started at Birmingham to Manchester Victoria, where 'Britannia' No 70013 *Oliver Cromwell* took the train to Carnforth. There, two BR Standard 4MT 4-6-0s, Nos 75027 and 75019, headed the train to Skipton. They are seen rounding the curve just south of Hellifield, in fine style. Two Class 5s, Nos 45073 and 45156, then hauled it to Rose Grove where 8F No 48773 took over for the trip back to Manchester Victoria via Copy Pit. **Date: 28 July 1968.**

◀ Long before No 45407 became the celebrity locomotive it is today, and probably the most widely travelled of any engine ever in the country, it was just another dirty Class 5 working out its time on unexciting duties. One regular working at the end of steam was the evening van train from Colne, which headed for Preston and called at most places en route. Here, it is at Accrington, on the side of the triangle connecting the line from the east with the one that used to head over Baxendale bank to Bury, before it reversed out of the station on to the viaduct and headed west. This was the last steam working of this train. **Date: 2 August 1968.**

⬆ The last Copy Pit banker passes into the history books, as it heads back to Rose Grove shed for the final time. The locomotive was 8F No 48278 and is seen near Portsmouth. It will have its fire dropped for the last time upon its return to the shed. **Date: 3 August 1968.**

➡ The last day of regular BR steam services had arrived and hundreds of enthusiasts descended on Preston station to see and travel on the last two trains, both hauled by Stanier Class 5s. The penultimate was the 20.50 to Blackpool South, part of the 17.05 ex-Euston, which is seen ready to depart with No 45212 in charge. It was followed by the very last working, which departed for Liverpool Exchange at 21.25, headed by No 45318, which was the 17.25 ex-Glasgow Central. Both were due to return to Lostock Hall shed but, after No 45212 returned light engine from Blackpool, it was put on carriage heating duties for the sleeper trains, and then continued on station pilot work into the afternoon of 4 August, thus it was claimed as becoming the last steam engine in normal BR service. Neither was selected to haul any of the last-day specials. No 45212 passed into preservation at the Keighley & Worth Valley Railway and has had periods of active service. News is now breaking that, after 45 years in preservation, having only served the LMS and BR for 33 years, it is to be returned to main line running in 2013. **Date: 3 August 1968.**

⬆ Deep inside Rose Grove shed, the evening sun shines on Class 5 No 45447 and 8F No 48393. Although the day was 10 June, both are recorded as being withdrawn on 4 August. The 8F had a slightly bent bufferbeam and the tracks behind No 45447 were very rusty, so I doubt if either ever steamed again. **Date: 10 June 1968.**

⬆ After travelling on the last BR regular steam train from Preston to Liverpool Exchange, I made my way back to Lostock Hall shed to find the place an absolute hive of activity, with enthusiasts busy cleaning the engines for the following day's last steam specials, with no BR staff present. My friends and I left at about 1am with many still hard at work. It must be said that, judging by the appearances of the locomotives the following day, the enthusiasts had done a terrific job. No 44894 is seen in the shed ready to haul 1Z78, one of the two Stephenson Locomotive Society specials the next day, with classmate No 44871. **Date: 4 August 1968.**

➡ Far too many slides were taken on Lostock Hall shed in the night, many of doubtful quality, but there was not going to be another chance again. No 45017 shows up well in the shed's lights, as it waits to be piloted the following day by No 44874 on 1Z79, the second Stephenson Locomotive Society special. **Date: 4 August 1968.**

There were six specials on 4 August, all running around the North West. Here, Class 5s Nos 44871 and 44894 are waiting for the arrival of 1Z78 from Birmingham, the first of the Stephenson Locomotive Society specials. This train was routed over Standedge to Huddersfield, up the Calder Valley main line, and over Copy Pit Summit to Blackburn. It then continued to Wigan Wallgate, Kirkby, Bootle, Stanley, and Rainhill to Manchester Victoria and then to Stockport, where an electric took over to Birmingham. **Date: 4 August 1968.**

I managed to photograph all six specials by rushing around, although a little more thought and care would have produced better results. By far the most memorable sight and sound of the day was the second SLS special, 1Z79, hauled by Class 5s Nos 44874 and 45017, as they tackled the last mile of the climb to Copy Pit Summit, when both the crews played to the assembled crowd and opened them up like I have never heard Class 5s worked before. This SLS special followed the same route as the first and so, a few hours after taking this shot, it was all over except for the '15 Guinea Special' on 11 August. **Date: 4 August 1968.**

↑ The dreaded 11 August arrived. The weather was good, so the last weekly Saturday or Sunday ritual of setting off to follow a 'last' steam special arrived. I decided to start with the '15 Guinea Special' near Guisburn and followed it without difficulty to Ribblehead, where this rather ordinary picture was taken. I then set off, fully expecting to catch it at Ais Gill, as I had done many times before, without realising that hundreds of others had decided to see it pass the summit. By the time I got the car parked, *Oliver Cromwell* must have been nearly at Carlisle. Two very poor pictures of the Class 5s were taken on the return trip, and so the curtain came down for the last time on BR steam, which proved to be a real anti-climax. **Date: 11 August 1968.**

→ During the last 12 months of BR steam, hundreds of enthusiasts travelled to the North West of the country to ride and photograph the dwindling workings. As sheds closed and there were fewer and fewer workings, it was not surprising that the areas they all went to became smaller and smaller, eventually resulting in a traffic jam at Ais Gill, the likes of which had probably never been seen in the Dales before, and possibly never will be again. Whilst the photographs of the special were very ordinary, the pictures of the traffic jam have turned out to be the most memorable, especially the cine film I took of the one solitary local policeman trying his best, against all the odds, to get the traffic away after the train had passed. **Date: 11 August 1968.**

Index

Classes index

Western Region

London Midland Region

55159 2P 0-4-4T Caledonian 4392 Class 12, 27
57230 2F 0-6-0 Caledonian 'Jumbo' 52

Eastern and North Eastern Regions

A1 4-6-2 79, 104
A2 4-6-2 110
A3 4-6-2 33-34, 56, 64-65
A4 4-6-2 9, 35, 66-67, 73, 90-91, 111, 140, 158
B1 4-6-0 15, 24-25, 51, 65, 149
B16 4-6-0 39
C14 4-4-2T 15
D16 4-4-0 10
D34 4-4-0 11
D49 4-4-0 10
J6 0-6-0 47
J21 0-6-0 17
J37 0-6-0 40-41, 100-102
J39 0-6-0 36, 41, 51

J50 0-6-0T 61
K1 2-6-0 22, 136, 150-151
K2 2-6-0 12, 23
K4 2-6-0 25
Q6 0-8-0 104
V2 2-6-2 72, 78, 158
Z4 0-4-2T 12

Southern Region

A1X 0-6-0T 'Terrier' 76-77
Beattie Well Tank 2-4-0T 77
E6 0-6-2T 77
K 2-6-0 45
LN 4-6-0 'Lord Nelson' 50
MN 4-6-2 2 'Merchant Navy' 117, 122-123, 141, 173
M7 0-4-4T 82
N15 4-6-0 'King Arthur' 49
O2 0-4-4T 76, 119
Q1 0-6-0 141, 159

S15 4-6-0 115
USA 0-6-0T 159
W 2-6-4T 45
WC 4-6-2 'West Country'/BB 4-6-2 'Battle of Britain' 48, 115-116, 118, 123, 142-143, 146, 160-161

British Railways Standards and WDs

70000 4-6-2 'Britannia' 87, 126, 138-139, 148-149, 171,176, 180-181, 187,191, 205
72000 4-6-2 'Clan' 21, 93
73000 4-6-0 5MT 24, 42, 185
75000 4-6-0 4MT 46, 145, 158, 162, 167-170, 183, 192-193, 200
76000 2-6-0 4MT 26, 79
77000 2-6-0 3MT 39, 79, 158
84000 2-6-2T 134
90000 2-8-0 'WD' 31, 53, 127, 162
92000 2-10-0 103, 155, 167, 172, 176-177, 184, 186

The End. Sunset at Rose Grove shed, August 1968.